Fortune Teller's Handbook

20 *Fun and Easy Techniques*
for Predicting the Future

Sasha Fenton

HAMPTON ROADS

Dedicated to the memory of my friend Gordon A. Smith, who has given me so much advice on psychic matters over the years.

Cover design by Jim Warner
Cover illustration: Alexander, crystal seer knows, sees, tells all.
circa 1910 © C. Alexander

Hampton Roads Publishing Company, Inc.
Charlottesville, VA 22906
Distributed by Red Wheel/Weiser, LLC
www.redwheelweiser.com

Sign up for our newsletter and special offers by going to
www.redwheelweiser.com/newsletter/.

ISBN: 978-1-57174-795-2

Library of Congress Cataloging-in-Publication Data available on request.

Printed in the United States of America
IBI
10 9 8 7 6 5 4 3 2 1

Contents

Introduction

Men and women have visited fortune tellers of one kind or another since the dawn of time. Even the most skeptical person enjoys an occasional reading, while many others visit a consultant at least once a year. There are hundreds of different methods of fortune telling, which range from highly developed skills to methods that simply prod the divinator's psychic awareness. Professional psychics know how to get the best from their spiritual guides because they have spent years studying and training in psychic development. A skilled astrologer, palmist, numerologist, tasseomancer, et al. is not really a fortune teller at all, but a combination of map reader, mathematician, and psychoanalyst. Not everyone however, wishes to devote his or her life to this kind of training; many people just want the fun and insight of being able to tell someone's fortune by a simple method of prediction.

This book investigates twenty different methods—all of them easy to understand and easy to use—as a means of introducing you to the mysteries of these ancient crafts. This book is meant to be very introductory, and most of all fun! These are all methods you can try out on yourself or with a group of friends.

These twenty chapters, however, are just the tip of the iceberg. In all cases, there are excellent and in-depth books available on the divination method in question, and I have provided a list of some in the further reading section at the end of this book for those who wish to move on to more serious study. There are a few methods included herein that, while intriguing, are a bit old fashioned or unusual—for example, phrenology and throwing witch doctor's bones. You may be able to find further information on these methods on the Internet.

Where necessary, I have drawn information for the divinations with which I am less familiar from other professionals, and I hope this brings these subjects to life and shows the reality of working in these fields rather than simply explaining the theories behind the methods. Where the information has come from other diviners and readers, I have used the term "querent" throughout to refer to the questioner, or the individual whose fortune is being read. I have mainly used the masculine terms "he" and "him" in order to keep the text simple. Fortune tellers and their clients are masculine, feminine, gay, straight, old, young, rich, poor, and from every country and culture in the world.

1

Numerology

This ancient method of divination is one of those that can be taken on a superficial level or it can be looked at very deeply. Numerology, like astrology, will give a good deal of information about a person's character as well as being helpful in predicting the pattern of trends and tendencies for the future. It is fascinating to work out and look at in the context of one's lifestyle at any given period of time. The numerologist, Fred Curtis, helped by giving me some useful information for this chapter.

The character of a name

The letters of your name need to be translated into a number system. Some numerologists insist that the name on a person's birth certificate should be used, but very few people use their name in that form. In my opinion, it makes more sense to use the name that you are happy and comfortable with rather than one your parents chose for you, and the name that you actually use should resonate properly with the person you are now. If you use a different name for your professional life than the one you use at home, try both and see what you get.

The alphabet code

Count up the numbers in your whole name, including middle name if used. Once you have done this, reduce the name to one digit. This will show you your basic character. The number represented by vowels represents your soul urge, while the personality you show to the outside world is shown by the consonants.

Example:

1	2	3	4	5	6	7	8	9
A	B	C	D	E	F	G	H	I
J	K	L	M	N	O	P	Q	R
S	T	U	V	W	X	Y	Z	

```
L I N D A T U L L E Y
3 9 5 4 1 2 3 3 3 5 7
```

Full name

Total numbers: = 45
Reduction: 4 + 5   = 9
Therefore Linda Tulley is a 9.

Vowels—soul urge

```
I A U E
9 1 3 5
```
Total numbers: = 18
Reduction: 1 + 8   = 9

Consonants—life lesson

```
L N D T L L Y
3 5 4 2 3 3 7
```
Total numbers: = 27
Reduction: 2 + 7   = 9

Linda Tulley therefore, has much the same feelings inside as those that she shows to the world. Her inner desires and her daily requirements are the same. She is an uncomplicated lady and she has reached a comfortable stage in her evolution.

Here is an example of someone far more complex:

Full name

```
F R A N K A N D E R S O N
6 9 1 5 2 1 5 4 5 9 1 6 5
```
Total numbers: = 59
Reduction: 5 + 9   = 14
Reduction: 1 + 4   = 5

Vowels

```
A A E O
1 1 5 6
```
Total numbers: = 13
Reduction: 1 + 3   = 4

Consonants

```
F R N K N D R S N
6 9 5 2 5 4 9 1 5
```
Total numbers: = 46
Reduction: 4 + 6   = 10
Reduction: 1 + 0   = 1

Frank projects an outward appearance of confidence and competence due to his consonant (1) while being basically a Mercurial type of person who has many interests and a need to communicate (5). He is reaching for security, a logical routine and method to his life, and a reliable inner world of stable relationships and finances that make some kind of realistic sense to him (4).

Naturally, there is more to numerology than this. Each letter has a value according to its position in the alphabet. An A for instance is more important than an E or an O.

The destiny number

The birth date shows the *destiny* for each person. It is also the birth date, in conjunction with any specific month or year, that is used for predicting trends and events.

Example one

Linda Tulley: July 17, 1946
Reduction: 7 + 1 + 7 + 1 + 9 + 4 + 6   = 35
Reduction: 3 + 5   = 8

Linda's life lesson is to cope with a structured and organized lifestyle that doesn't leave much time for personal freedom or pleasure. Poor Linda. The fact is that Linda is the wife of a successful businessman who works in the building trade. She helps him a little with the paperwork but she is also fully occupied with her job as a registered daycare center owner. She has four sons, and she is the first to admit that her fourth pregnancy was not planned and that her life is extremely busy and highly structured. Linda occasionally resents the fact that she rarely gets to leave her large house and that she has little time for herself.

Example two

Frank Anderson: March 3, 1935
Reduction: 3 + 2 + 7 + 1 + 9 + 3 + 5   = 30
Reduction: 3 + 0   = 3

Frank's life lesson is to have the courage to grow and develop in a creative manner and also to cope with success and material gain. However, Frank's soul urge being a highly structured 4 makes this hard for him. He needs fun, humor, and to be able to own and enjoy things of value without feeling guilty. He needs to develop sensitivity and to control the more obstinate or awkward sides of his personality.

The Character of Each Number

Start by taking the number in the whole name for an overview of a person's character, and then look at their soul urge and life lesson numbers. In the case of our example of Frank Anderson, this would mean checking out the numbers 5, 4 and 1.

Number One

 The number one relates to the self and also to the conscious, rational, reasoning mind. Any achievement needs to be preceded by a thought before it can be translated into action. The number one stands alone. It is bold, powerful, and it is a force that translates energy into matter. It has strongly masculine qualities. This number is pioneering, the first in line, dominant, original, and independent. The downside is that this leads to domineering and selfish behavior that can easily turn to aggression. It is wonderful when this person uses his powers of invention to get things done, to better himself to help others, and to protect those he loves. However, if he uses it to bully others, he won't get very far in love or working relationships.

This number shows that the person may have been dominated and bullied as a child. One or both parents may have thought they were always right, possibly due to their religious beliefs. They put pressure upon the youngster to perform or conform to their ideal. The upside of this is that the subject turns into a hard working and ambitious type who is especially suited to self-employment or to reaching the top in a profession. The downside is that the number one person may copy his parents' pattern and seek to dominate others in his turn. Alternatively, he may become anxious and fearful of the future. If he can find someone who will love him and give him the emotional support that he needs, he can overcome this. He would not only become successful in life, but others would value him for his honesty, generosity, humor, and sense of adventure.

Number Two

 This number implies duality. It represents the womb-like quality of nurturing a seed that has been planted by the number one energy. It represents a drive for harmony and balance, a need for a feminine yin to balance the masculinity of yang. It is passive, intuitive, receptive, and emotional. This number indicates partnerships and relationships, so the chances are that these will be important to the person.

There may have been considerable tensions in the childhood home, and this leads this person to develop a hard shell in order to protect himself. Childhood events may result in the kind of insecurity that he relieves by becoming penny-pinching and miserly. He may seek to acquire goods in order to make himself feel safe. Even if he doesn't go to this extreme, he will probably always be careful with money and possessions. He is very keen on family life and he will be fiercely loyal to his loved ones and will even carry the habit of loyalty through to his employers. He is not a natural leader, because he prefers to help others and to be appreciated for what he does. He may choose to work in one of the caring professions.

Number Three

This is a creative number, so it represents creative enterprise and growth. The seed that was planted in a number one year and nurtured during a number two year is now showing signs of growth. This number suggests that material benefits will eventually come to this person.

This person may be quite artistic or he may have literary talents, but he may not have been encouraged to express this during his youth, so this may lead to frustration. This subject probably found it difficult to stand up to his parents and he may have a problem with authority figures throughout life. The result is that he may be stubborn and irritable when dealing with others, or too charming and accommodating. Despite a difficult start, he usually does well in his chosen profession. He may also be extremely lucky in his choice of friends and colleagues, and these people may be happy to help him whenever they can. He is sociable and flirtatious, he enjoys having a good time and also seeing others enjoy themselves.

Number Four

Four signifies the earth and the physical and material world. It represents a foundation that a person can build upon. Number four is the number of form and common sense, reason, and control over the energies that are at one's command. Four represents balance, stability, and security, but it also symbolizes restrictions and limitations. Logical thinking and systematic work methods belong to this number.

This subject's childhood should have been a happy one with plenty of love and support from family and teachers. He may get into the habit later in life of leaning on others and treating them as replacement parents or teachers. He will always be a hard and reliable worker with a sensible attitude to whatever he takes on. He is loyal and sensitive to those he loves. He is a loyal employee, although he can also succeed in a business of his own. He may be a little unimaginative, but he makes an excellent financial advisor or craftsman, and his capacity for hard work earns rewards. He is a loyal and loving family person.

Number Five

 The number five shows the need to break out of the enclosed structure that is signified in the number four. This number breeds activity because it hates routine and restriction, and it becomes very nervous and restless when held down. It hates to see its freedom threatened because it needs a wide area in which to move around and to express its drive and energy. The number five seeks constant change and variety, and the scope to put the fruits of physical and mental experiences into action. This number is associated with social contacts, education, ideas, and communications of all kinds.

This person's parents were reasonable and his childhood was fairly happy, but there were events that made him feel very insecure. His parents may have been sick, they may have been refugees of some kind, or they may just have moved around a lot, which meant that the subject had to go through several changes of home or school. He may tend to walk away from problems rather than face them. His desire for the admiration of others may lead him to become a success in sports or the media. He is clever and versatile; he needs variety in his life and a number of different challenges in his job. He enjoys moving around and meeting a variety of different people in his working and social life or talking on the phone much of the time. He accepts the ideas of others, but he can be a good leader because he allows others to do their jobs without undue interference. He cannot have a relationship with a boring partner.

Number Six

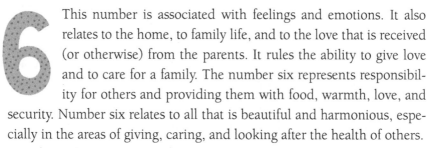 This number is associated with feelings and emotions. It also relates to the home, to family life, and to the love that is received (or otherwise) from the parents. It rules the ability to give love and to care for a family. The number six represents responsibility for others and providing them with food, warmth, love, and security. Number six relates to all that is beautiful and harmonious, especially in the areas of giving, caring, and looking after the health of others.

This subject will have felt extremely insecure when young and he may have had parents who either did not communicate or who gave him strangely mixed messages. His mother may have had some sensible things to say at times, but also some very fixed ideas that may not have been normal or logical. His family venerated hard work and he may have sought to impress them and to win their approval by working hard—even as a child. The outcome is that he becomes a tireless worker in adult life, possibly wearing himself out for the sake of others. If his family and employers appreciate and value him for the effort that he makes, he will feel that he has achieved all that he set out to do. His chief fault is perfectionism. This subject's mind is excellent and he does much to help others, often through a genuine desire to make the world a better place to live.

Number Seven

This number represents two linked ideas. The first is the need for rest, relaxation, and time off to think things through, or just to allow thoughts to drift around aimlessly. After a while, the thoughts take shape and something useful will emerge. The second idea is that of spiritual significance, as this encompasses the kind of reflection, analysis, and inward journey that leads to enlightenment of both a practical and spiritual nature. In essence, this is a meditative number.

This person probably had a fairly easy-going relationship with parents and other adults, partly because he is reasonable, sociable, and pleasant. He turns his amiable nature to good advantage both in his career and his personal relationships, but he needs to guard against a tendency to let opportunities pass him by. This subject must avoid sitting back and allowing others to make progress at his expense or to take what should rightfully be his. He prefers thinking to acting and he tends to sit back and observe the world and all that goes on there. He may become a philosopher, a mystic, or an artist. He is wise, but he may not cash in on his talents and wisdom or achieve much. If he can develop his artistic talents and find a practical life partner, he will find that the world appreciates him.

Number Eight

 This number suggests material success but also spiritual attainment. There has to be progress in both areas and a balance needs to be maintained between them. This karmic number shows that we reap what we sow. The number eight also indicates a mastery over the physical world and an acceptance of responsibility.

If your destiny number is eight, your childhood will not have been easy, either because you were rebellious and disinclined to conform, or because one or both of your parents was domineering, dictatorial, or rigid. You may have dealt with this by defying your parents or by using cunning and sly behavior to get what you wanted. Either way, you learn to use charm later in life to get what you want. You are extremely intuitive and you can sum up people and situations almost in a flash. Add this to your sharp intelligence, your organizational ability, and your capacity for hard work, and it is easy to see that you will make a tremendous success of your chosen career. You are the one who will end up with wealth and status. You may become domineering yourself in later life and you may see even your personal relationships as a kind of power struggle. If you can curb your sharp tongue and learn to be tolerant of those who are not lucky enough to be born with your strength and courage, you can make your loved ones happy and in turn become happy yourself. You need to ease up a little and learn to relax and enjoy life.

Number Nine

 This incorporates all the previous numbers, so it represents completion and true love of the highest order. This shows that a certain point has been reached although there are always higher levels to aspire to. Listening to our inner voices and working by divine standards are the only paths to success. In this case, the soul may be old, but there is always something more to learn.

If you are a nine-destiny person, your parents were keen for you to do well and you could go on to prove them right by becoming a success. You have an inner urge for exploration, and this could take you into the realms of education or hobbies and interests that give you an opportunity to look at things from a variety of different angles. In many cases, the visionary aspect of your nature can lead to an involvement in religion, philosophy, or the spiritual life, and you can inspire others. Travel is a strong theme in your life, and you could end up seeing a fair bit of the world. You use your ability to get on with all manners of people to bring you success in business, but there is a side of your nature that could lead you to simply drift along without getting very much anywhere.

• • •

Although numerology normally uses the numbers from one to nine, the numbers eleven, twenty-two, and thirty-three are also used when assessing a person's character.

Number Eleven

The energy behind this number is of justice, fair play, and of strength that is used wisely. There are times when it is right to administer justice but others when it is right just to sit back and wait things out. The trick is to know which is which.

As a destiny number, eleven suggests that your childhood might have been reasonable, but something made you determined to keep yourself to yourself. You may have been distrustful of adults or of other children or disinclined to listen to anything that others had to say. You seem to have been a quiet and rather serious child. In later life, you could become opinionated, inflexible and difficult. You may develop a terrific inferiority complex, which you hide under an arrogant, uncaring or defiant attitude. If you find the right career outlet for your talents and develop sensitivity toward others, you may overcome your natural tendency for self-absorption. You have an original mind and you are attracted to unconventional ideas and an unconventional lifestyle. Marriage, children and a routine family life may never appeal to you.

Number Twenty-two

There is an element of justice that must be applied here. You may receive just or unjust treatment during the course of your life but you should always strive to be fair in your dealings with others. There is a feeling of completion here, with just rewards for all that you have done before (perhaps in a previous life).

If your destiny number is twenty-two, you both loved and admired your parents or feared their strength and domination. You grew up to become an independent person with an unusual outlook or nonconformist attitude. You understand the underlying motives of others. You also have an uncanny feel for the structure of materials and this could lead you to become a builder, civil engineer, architect, or creative artist. You also make an excellent counselor and guide to younger people. If you can control your tendency toward angry or wounding outbursts, you can succeed in a relationship, especially one with a partner who needs to be guided and cared for.

Number Thirty-three

33 This is a difficult number in which loneliness and hardship will occur, but these experiences bring enlightenment and an ability to sympathize with the plight of others. Charitable work, doing things for others and self-sacrifice have a part to play here, but there is also the development of a strong inner world of spirituality and artistry.

If this is your destiny number, you may have been somewhat isolated during your childhood, possibly due to sickness and spells in the hospital, and this leads you to develop your creativity and imagination. Later in life when storms threaten, you can escape into a dream world of your own making. Your parents were not particularly hard on you, but life and circumstances made you a little fearful. You will probably end up in one of the caring professions. You might take up spiritual work where you spend your life helping and giving yourself to others. The danger here is that you become overtaken by the needs of others and that you expend your energies, leaving you drained and exhausted. If necessary, you can be practical and very successful, but you probably will always want to help others. If you can develop your artistic talents and work quietly on your own projects, you can achieve considerable success.

Personal Month or Year Fortunes

It is easy to discover your fortune for a particular year. All you need to do is to add the numbers of the day and month of your birth to the year as a whole. For example, if you were born on September the 2nd and you want to look at 2004, this would mean adding $9 + 2 + 2 + 0 + 0 + 4$ to make 16 which then reduces to the number 7.

If you want to look at the first four months of the year, add your *whole name* number to the year in question. For the middle four months, add the *life lesson* number, and for the last four months, add the *soul urge* number.

It is worth bearing in mind that, while a number *one* year indicates a fresh start for any person, any year or any part of a year that is the same as your destiny number is bound to be important.

A number one year

Key ideas: Beginning, initiative, decisions, and individuality.

This is the start of a new phase, so if you apply it to a whole year, what you do now will determine the pattern of events for the following nine years. If you apply it to a four month period, this sets the tone for the next few months. You may feel quite alone during this year even if family and friends surround you, and you may wonder how you are going to make it on your own. You need to decide how you are going to operate your life and to make decisions that should determine your future course. This is a period in which you set things in place, although you may not be able to get them off the ground in quite the way that you would like just yet. In some ways, this is a period of adjustment in which you may find yourself coping with a new way of life.

You will feel surges of energy and a desire to do things for yourself. This may be a matter of personal choice or it may be that you find yourself alone and unsupported. You won't want to accept defeat, because you will feel that your instincts are right. It would be a good idea to take time out on occasion to reflect and to listen to your intuition and also to heed sensible advice. You will find it necessary to put yourself first at this time and to set your own plans into action.

You will shed old problems and any lingering timidity will vanish. There will be new methods of work to get to grips with and new ways of looking at old problems. Important people may come into your life at this time and they may act mentors or teachers. Be discriminating in your choice of friends at this time because alliances that are made now will last. This is the time to stand up for what you believe in, to be self-reliant, self-motivated, and independent.

A number two year

Key ideas: Cooperation, partnerships, creativity, peace, harmony, and peaceful coexistence.

You will need to work in harmony with others and you will need to be aware of their requirements. You may need to take a slightly passive role and to be diplomatic when handling other people. You may be called upon to judge situations on behalf of others and to settle disputes. Partnership matters will be important but so will personal creativity. You will find that you have useful flashes of inspiration.

This is not a good time to make major decisions, and if things become unstable it will be best to keep going and to remain passive while allowing things to take their course. Love affairs may become unsettled due to hidden factors and underlying problems, however you can work on these in order to improve them. You may uncover some kind of deception around you or discover secret enemies who work against you. If others are not honest with you, at least be honest with yourself. Try to take time out to relax and to tune into your own intuition, as this will be your best guide at such times.

A number three year

Key ideas: Activity, expansion, travel, creativity and self-expression.

You may feel the urge to travel within your own country or overseas—either way you will feel the need to move around freely and to explore. Take the opportunity to do so because this will prove to be a mind-broadening experience. New faces and new horizons will enable you to assess yourself in a different light.

This is a year of activity and social events in which you will make yourself the center of attention. The new exposure will make you take a fresh look at yourself and you may wish to change your image or appearance. It is important that you look good because a good appearance and a confident manner will impress those who you come into contact with. This could be an unusually lucky period in which you may win as a result of entering competitions or even gambling. Business opportunities are also in the air now.

There may be a new baby in your circle during this period, and there will certainly be new and far more creative projects to get your teeth into at this time. Be sure that the enthusiasm, optimism, and expansion don't lead to extravagance, wastefulness, and loss. Over-indulgence might lead to weight gain. The domestic scene could prove troublesome, possibly because you will be busy elsewhere. If you scatter your time and energies too much, you will lose your effectiveness. If you drift along and make no effort, this could be a wasted year, but if you make an effort to carry your ideas through in a constructive manner, this could be one of the happiest years of your life.

A number four year

Key ideas: Work, law and order, budgeting, foundations, sex, and regeneration or recycling in some way.

This is a time to concentrate on work on the material plane. You may be so determined to organize your life that you clear out the attic, cellar, cupboards, desks, drawers, and the garage. You will be driven by a subconscious desire to build a firm and secure foundation, so you will tidy up your environment and put your affairs in order.

Everything relating to money and possessions will become important now, and it is essential that you make your life secure and stable, so you will need to budget carefully. This number highlights land, property, building, and renovations, so you could find yourself involved in extra expense in this area of your life. Take care of your money, and it will take care of you. Your body is your home as well, so the extravagances and excesses of the previous cycle will make you keen to get back into shape. As all the physical senses become heightened, your current sexual relationship should be come rewarding and stimulating. Males could decide to father children now.

This number relates to law and order so you must be sure to behave honestly in all your dealings. You may well be on the way to business success now, so this is a good time to buy material goods and possessions. Enjoy this by all means, but don't become a slave to possessions—own them and don't allow them to own you. Also pay attention to the health and finances of your family. You may become stubborn and oversensitive at this time.

A number five year

Key ideas: Communication, decisions, change, experience, sexuality.

There is so much activity in your life at the moment that you will find it hard to keep up the pace. You are totally involved in attending meetings, running errands, answering the telephone, making arrangements, and going to parties and social functions that you feel as though you are on a merry-go-round.

This is a period of communication and education, so gaining experience and making contacts will be your most important activity now. You need to look closely at your life and to choose the right direction because change is in the air. If you are dissatisfied with your current situation, this is the time to do something about it. New doors will open to you and new solutions to your problems will present themselves.

This is the year in which the opposite sex suddenly discovers you. Your calendar will be filled, you will become the life and soul of any party, and admirers will surround you. This activity will include travel, so ensure that your vehicle is in tip-top order and that your gas tank is full. Your nervous system will be at full stretch, so it might be advisable to avoid too much alcohol and keep away from drugs. You need to be in top gear rather than zonked out on some opiate. You may feel that you are wasting your energies on superficial relationships, but this is probably not the time for commitment. You may need light-hearted love affairs for what they can teach you.

This is not a year for routine activities, and you will need to be free to take off at a moment's notice. Indeed, there will be several unexpected and very pleasant events. You may feel resentful toward those who seek to hold you back or keep you down, and this may encourage you to break away from stultifying relationships. Without change, there is no growth, but you still need some underlying goal to focus upon so that you don't simply fritter this year away in aimless pleasure seeking.

A number six year

Key ideas: Duty, responsibility, love, home, family, justice, beauty, and emotional matters.

During a number six year, the emphasis is usually on the home and family. There may be changes in the home with new people entering the family while others leave. Responsibilities within the home will increase. This year number is associated with marriage but it can also indicate divorce, and this is because you will seek a balance in this area of your life. During the restless phase of the previous year, you may have experimented with new relationships, and you may begin to feel that you are ready to cope with a settled relationship and to establish a home.

Beauty will become an issue, both as it relates to your own appearance and also to that of your surroundings. You might decorate your home and you will certainly take more care of your appearance. You are so tuned into the need for balance that you could become a peacemaker, and you could even take up counseling in a professional capacity. Some legal decisions will occur and these will also be aimed at restoring balance and harmony.

If balance cannot be restored, separations will occur and differences will become irreconcilable—either in your personal life or in the business arena. Try to settle arguments with fairness, and try to show understanding toward your loved ones during this period. This is a year of duty to others, both within the home and at work, so the only way to get anywhere is to work hard and do what has to be done.

A number seven year

Key ideas: Rest, perfection, health, analysis.

This is a period of retreat. You may feel more tired than usual and you may not wish to socialize. You need time alone to think, meditate, reflect, and analyze matters and to go on an inward journey. It is a good time to take weekends off or vacations by the sea or in the countryside. Try to set material worries aside now and don't push yourself too hard. Do the work that is on hand and don't take on anything more. Leave goals and ambitions alone for a while because if you work too hard at this time you will make yourself ill.

This is a good time to take a course of study and it may be that mind, body, and spirit subjects grab your attention, as you are in a particularly receptive frame of mind at this time. You may experience interesting dreams, visions, and psychic events. The fact is that you have spent the last few years getting your body, home, work, family, and finances into shape, so this is a good time to take things easier and to concentrate on spiritual matters.

A number eight year

Key ideas: Karma, responsibility, strength, business, service to others, sex, balance, and harmony.

Now the truth of everything becomes clear and karma reigns. The law of cause and effect will bring you what you have earned or what you deserve. For some, this means advancement in your career, a higher salary, public recognition, honor, awards, and even legacies. For others there will be hardship, material loss, unemployment, and possibly even bankruptcy. The emphasis will be on the more serious aspects of finance and security. Pressures and responsibilities at work will mount and you will feel the strain of the extra work load, although this may come as a result of promotion or of starting something new. Additional money will be available and you may even receive an inheritance, so your bank balance should be healthier. However, the negative aspect could include job loss, business failure, and financial burdens. Either way, pressure and responsibility become key issues.

Intense sexual relationships are possible now and this could also be wrapped up with responsibility for others. A relationship may feel like heaven on earth. Whatever the prevailing financial situation, you and your partner will pull together during this phase. If you allow the loss of material possessions to get you down or get so bent on gaining more possessions that you start to dominate others, you will become unhappy. Whatever your circumstances, a balance between the material and spiritual world will need to be found.

A number nine year

Key ideas: Endings, transition, charity, friendships, and wisdom.

This is the last year of a nine-year cycle, so your fortune has turned full circle and you are almost back to the beginning again, so you are preparing for the wheel to make another revolution. If you have been operating in harmony with the universe, you will have gained much experience and knowledge over the past nine years. If your life has been out of balance, then you will have experienced loss, heartache, and upheaval. Now is the time to find the right spiritual values, greater understanding, a stronger mental attitude, and spiritual awareness.

This is the time to let go of outworn values, to give up those associations that have no place in your life or future. People may leave your life, or you may change your career or relocate your home and leave some people or things to which you are attached. The status quo will be upset. If you find change and transformation difficult, this will be an emotionally trying time. You may feel like crying at times, and you will need to retreat from life at times and reflect on your situation. You will come into contact with your inner self. When endings occur, it is because there is something new around the corner and when one door closes, another opens. Try to be aware of this and to accept changes willingly because ultimately, they will be for your own good. Use some of your energies in charitable deeds, and give back to the universe some of what you have gained.

You should not try to work alone now, but join with others for the common good. Be sympathetic, compassionate, understanding, and loving to those whom you encounter during this cycle. Old friendships can become especially meaningful and heart-warming, while beautiful new relationships can develop.

Negatively, some people become overemotional during a number nine vibration, and they refuse to listen or even try to understand what is going on. If you try to cling to those things that you can no longer have, you simply prolong a transition period and also prolong the pain. Don't look back to past insecurities, look to the future. You cannot change the past but you will soon have an opportunity to mold the future.

2

Flower Reading

Gordon A. Smith gave me the information for this section of this book. Gordon is a psychic medium, healer, and card reader who has been involved with the world of spirituality for many years and he is much respected for his knowledge. Like many of my friends, Gordon has held many posts on the committee of the British Astrological and Psychic Society, including being chairman on and off over the years.

The method

Flower reading is an unusual form of divination that I hadn't come across until Gordon demonstrated it for me. It requires a good deal of intuition and psychic perception. The querent should choose the flower and bring it to the reader for interpretation. The flower should be left to rest in a vase or on a piece of tissue until the reader is ready to begin. The reader then picks up the flower and reads it from the bottom of the stem up to the top of the bloom. The bottom of the stem represents the querent's childhood while the stem and bloom represent the path of a person's life and his future. The following list shows how to interpret various parts of the flower:

- A roughly torn stem indicates a difficult childhood. A smoothly cut one suggests an easy start to life.

- Smooth sections of stalk indicate smooth periods of life, whereas rough, torn, or discolored patches denote times of trouble. Discolored patches suggest marriage or relationship problems.

- New branches bring new beginnings, while a division of the stem denotes choices and different pathways that could be taken.

- Buds that come to nothing suggest losses or situations that don't work out.

- A new shoot or a group of leaves at the appropriate age can indicate the birth of children.

- Strong leaves represent living children, while weak ones that fizzle out denote miscarriages or even losses in infancy.

- Illness may be indicated by a weak patch such as thinning or twisting of the stalk.

- The bloom shows whether the querent will achieve his current ambitions. A bud represents desires and ideas that have yet to be achieved, whereas an open flower will show success and achievement of goals.

- Friends and relatives are represented by leaves. The reader must look at the leaves and judge their condition in order to see how these people will affect the querent.

- Career matters that are coming into being will be highlighted by a bud, but when these are in top gear, a bloom will denote this. When coming to an end, there will be a bunch of dying petals.

- Anything that is curling up or dying shows that some part of the querent's life is wending its way to a conclusion. Anything that has been attacked by insects is under attack by others or by forces outside the querent's control.

- Thorns symbolize knotty problems.

As you can see, this kind of reading is open to interpretation by the individual reader, but when added to some psychic ability, it works surprisingly well. Certainly the sample reading that Gordon gave was very successful, and he picked up a number of facts about my past that he could not have known and he also correctly identified a couple of major career decisions that were on my mind at the time of the reading.

He actually told me that an important offer would come to me from overseas when the flower was in full bloom. Over the succeeding days, the bud opened, the flower bloomed and then died. I threw it out with a shrug of my shoulders, but a few days later I received an important offer from Australia—and the letter had been posted on the day when the flower was in full bloom!

3

The Crystal Ball

When a client visits a crystal ball reader, his eyes tell him that there is a solid glass ball with nothing visible inside it, but judging by what the reader tells him, he assumes that there must be something there! So what is crystal reading? How is it done? Can anyone do it? I put these questions to two friends of mine who use their crystal balls in two completely different ways, and this was the result.

Robin Lown

Robin is a palmist, Tarot reader, clairvoyant and crystal reader and he is on the committee of the British Astrological and Psychic Society. This side of his life exists in addition to him having a "proper job" as an inspector of schools within the British education system. This is what Robin had to tell me about crystal gazing.

Setting the scene

If you want to buy a crystal ball, visit a psychic festival or a shop specializing in these things and have a good look at what is available. Weigh the crystals that you like in your hand and see which ones you feel drawn to, because the shape and size is important. You may even fancy a colored crystal for your readings. Never buy any item of this nature by mail order because you need to try it to see if it feels right. Having said this, most professionals seem to have had their crystals given to them or bought for them, or they seem to have acquired their crystal in some odd way.

Before trying to use your crystal, wash it thoroughly in spring water and leave it out in the sun to dry, then meditate on it, asking for it to work for you and also to bring help and guidance to those who consult you. I charged my own crystal by holding it in my hands within my aura and telling the spirit world that I wanted to use it in order to give help, service and truth to those who needed it. I meditated on it as being part of myself, reaffirming myself as a seeker of truth. Even now when using my crystal, my motives have to be clear. I must want to be of service and help to the querent because any other feelings would disrupt the reading, and I would have to start over again. Most people respect the crystal for what it is and ask permission before picking it up. I have noticed that only crass materialists and those who are totally unaware of spiritual matters attempt to pick it up without asking permission, and I am afraid that I get quite testy with them when this happens.

How do I read?

I use palmistry first (see chapter 20) in order to create a link with the querent, then I give them the crystal to hold. I tell them that is it not necessary for them to think of anything in particular. After this, I ask for the crystal back and I place it on a stand, which is on a piece of black cloth. Then I slowly tune in. I use the crystal as a form of psychometry and I don't think that I actually see anything in the crystal itself. Rather, I see images that are projected from my head in a kind of psychic ventriloquism and a projection of what is in my mind. First, I see scenes, people, and situations, and then I begin to feel impressions and emotions. My method is definitely allied to psychometry, clairvoyance, clairaudience, and clairsentience.

(I asked Robin whether crystal reading had ever lead him to mediumistic experiences where he was in contact with friends or relatives of the querent who had "passed over." He said that this did happen on occasion and that there were also times when he felt himself being "taken over" by someone who wanted to express his or her thoughts through him.)

At this point, I obviously don't know whether the images that I see are of the past, present, or future, so I inwardly ask my Guiding Spirit to tell me. I ask whether this is the past and then wait until I get a yes or no feeling. If the event turns out to be in the past, I ask to be shown what relevance this might have to the present—and this often brings another image to me. By now, I will be aware that my Chakras* are open and that both the crystal and the querent are within my auric bubble. I then start to tell the querent what I am receiving. As he or she begins to connect with what I am saying, the images and impressions speed up and become more definite, more certain—and then it becomes much easier for me. Sometimes a querent can block me, either because he is skeptical or for some other reason. Then I see or feel only a shaft of light, as though it were coming down a tunnel, at which point I give up and resort to reading the querent's palm or cards, both of which are less subject to psychic disturbance.

I then asked Robin how long he would spend on a reading like this, and he said that it depended upon the rapport that he had with the querent and the amount of information that came through. He told me that he always finished a reading by giving a summary of the main points as he saw them. He also kept a pencil and a pad of paper nearby so that he could sketch an item if he wanted to (Robin is artistic). He also told me that he tended to see certain particular symbols as his centers were opening up. One of them was the figure of eight symbol for infinity that appears over the Magician's head in the Tarot deck, the other was the caduceus, which is the winged staff carried by the Roman god, Mercury, which signifies enlightenment, healing abilities, and magical powers.

---

*The Chakras are the seven psychic centers in the body that have to open up in order to allow psychic impressions to flow in and out.

Barbara Ellen

Barbara is a full-time professional clairvoyant and medium. She is also a consultant for the British Astrological and Psychic Society. Barbara has had many years of experience; she is highly trained and very skilled and knowledgeable. Although Barbara is not primarily a crystal gazer (she tells me that she finds pure clairvoyance quicker and easier), she can use a crystal ball very well when she is required to do so. This is what Barbara told me.

Preparing a new crystal ball

It is far better to acquire a crystal than to buy a new one—another reader gave mine to me years ago. Wherever your crystal has come from, the first thing you need to do is to immerse it for twelve hours in salted spring water. Some readers use a solution of vinegar and water. After this, wash the crystal under running water, ideally from some natural source such as a waterfall or a stream. If you haven't access to a stream, find something that will collect fresh rain water and then allow the water to flow over the ball. Polish the crystal with a chamois leather and leave it in the sunlight for at least four hours. After that, don't ever allow anyone else to touch or even to look into your crystal.

Training and preparation

Some readers spin the crystal with a finger while they are tuning themselves in, while many others work from mental impressions (as Robin does), but I try to use the crystal itself as it should be used.

Place the crystal on a small plinth that is covered by a black cloth. Ideally the cloth should be silk because this is a completely natural product, although many readers prefer to use velvet because it has a denser texture. Partially cover or surround the crystal with a second black cloth, which

should definitely be made of silk. If you wish, you can darken the room slightly and put on a dim light. Some readers use a red light as this is known to draw the spirit world close. Practice sessions should always be carried out at the same time of the day and never late at night—this procedure seems to help our spiritual guides to work better. Cup the crystal in the cloth and bring it up so that it is in front of your forehead—that is close, but not touching the "third eye," which is in the center of your forehead. While training, you must keep the crystal within your aura. This means keeping it wrapped in its silk or velvet cloth on a table next to you while you sleep, read, or watch television, or in a bag at your side while out and about. Never try to read on a full stomach or if you are upset or angry. Do some yoga breathing each time before you start training or reading. To do this, breath in from the stomach for a count of four, hold the breath for a count of two and let it out on a count of four. Do this exercise four times. Relax, get yourself into a peaceful state of mind and then go ahead.

If you begin to see symbols in the crystal during this time, note them down. You may be aware of certain symbols that are personal to you such as a black cat, a white rabbit, and so on. Keep a note of what these mean and build up a vocabulary of signs and symbols.

The crystal should begin to cloud and it is important that when this happens that you remain calm and don't let yourself become overexcited or the vision will disappear. Red or orange "smoke" is a warning of danger; blue or green "smoke" is fine. Objects that are colored red or orange are another thing altogether, because only red "smoke" warns you to be on the alert. The visions will go out of focus and then come back sharply into focus, but you will have to wait a few minutes for this to happen— perhaps as long as five minutes. This training period will last for about eight days but you must persevere with it until the ability comes. When an image comes, wait for the message that comes with it. This message will come into your mind through the help of your Spiritual Guides. Sometimes the objects will come into view first and the clouds later, because every reader works slightly differently. Be sure to ask your Spiritual Guides to help you.

When I see images moving in the crystal, I know that those that come in from the left represent events that are coming toward the querent while those on or travelling toward the right are passing away from him. This is how it works for me, but you may see things or do things differently.

As soon as you feel that you are making a link with your crystal, either with mental pictures or actually seeing milky-type smoke or images within the ball itself, find some guinea pigs to sit for you. Try to find people who you know nothing about. Ask your querent to cup his or her hands around the crystal without actually touching it and to remain in that position for approximately two minutes. Then take the crystal back from the querent and relax. Shade the crystal from the light and begin to give out whatever comes. As soon as your sitter can acknowledge that you are getting something meaningful through, it will come through even more quickly. Any kind of feedback will help. Be sure to keep notes so that you can assess your progress and make adjustments in your thinking.

A Sample Reading

At this point Barbara went on to give me a reading. I hadn't expected this, so it was an unaccustomed treat. The first thing that she saw was an airplane. This was not surprising as I traveled a lot at that time and I was due to take a trip to New York at the time of the reading. She then saw my son Stuart waving a document of some kind. Stuart was about to take an exam in computer and business studies. Barbara also told me that she could see my husband with a pain in his back and leg. This was not surprising as my then husband, Tony Fenton, had been doing some heavy work and his back was never strong at the best of times. She then told me that my daughter, Helen, needed new glasses. As it happened, Helen had recently had some new specs so that didn't make much sense at the time, but it turned out a few days later that the prescription was wrong and the shop had to make up replacement lenses for her.

4

Fortune Telling by Dice

It is a fact that anything that has specific numbers, letters, shapes, colors, denominations, or anything else of a regular nature can be used for fortune telling. As long as you assign a particular meaning to each number, letter, shape, or color and stick to it, this will work for you. The list below is the way that I would interpret the numbers on the dice, but if you have a favorite system of your own, please feel free to use it.

The method

The simplest method is to use three dice of any size or color. Hold them in your hands for a moment and concentrate on whatever is on your mind—if you wish, you could even blow on the dice. Throw the dice gently onto a table and see what comes up.

If you wish to make things a little more interesting, you can take a pretty piece of card and draw a design on it. The design should contain seven areas or segments that the dice can easily fall into. The following suggestions cover the kind of thing that most people are keen to ask about, these are *health, family life, relationships, money, career, property, and pot luck.* The pot luck area can be used for anything that is outside the six basic items.

You can draw a flower with several petals, something that looks Indian or Egyptian, or a series of simple circles or rectangles that are arranged in a group or even within one another—it can be as simple or as artistic as you wish to make it. Then see which segments are activated by the dice and direct your reading accordingly.

The List of Meanings

One

A new beginning, the start of something important and a feeling of rebirth. Sometimes this indicates the actual birth of a child.

Two

This indicates a partnership that might be business or personal, and while this will need work and perhaps a little caution, it should be successful. A separation is also possible, or perhaps this is a kind of splitting of resources or of two things that move into two different locations.

Three

This represents a celebration, joy, perhaps a wish that is fulfilled and good news. Sometimes there is sadness, loss, or sickness.

Four

This indicates financial and domestic security and putting down roots, also rest and recuperation after a period of hard work or after illness. This should be fine, but sometimes there is a feeling that while much is satisfactory, something more needs to be done.

Five

This is a difficult number that shows trouble and strife, arguments, losses, and sickness. Sometimes there is a period of challenge or a time of hard work that works out well. There may be travel in connection with business and sometimes also a little time off to enjoy sports, games, and even a little gamble.

Six

This might take you back into a past situation. Alternatively, you may need to abandon the past and look for something completely new. Sometimes this involves travel or relocating, but it can also symbolize a feeling of moving away from trouble and into a more successful environment. There may be a feeling of victory and achievement.

Seven

There will be plenty to do, but you can only cope with this if you break it down into workable segments. Muddles will come to an end and you will soon be able to decide on what to keep and what you wish to abandon.

There will be slow growth and development and slow moves forward. Seek out legal or professional advice if necessary.

Eight

This signifies a time when life speeds up. There may be fresh opportunities, a new job, travel, and perhaps a new address or environment. There may be something that holds you back, but this seems to be more a case of fear of change or a reluctance to make the effort than a real problem.

Nine

This number suggests happy family life, comfort, a happy home life, satisfaction, safety, and money. However, there may also some kind of worry or heartache due to a family problem.

Ten

Either great success in all things (money, love, health, career, etc.) or if other omens are poor, there can be a complete collapse of plans or even a stab in the back.

Eleven

This can refer to children, young people, or even vague friendships. Otherwise, it relates to news and small events that can lead to larger and more important ones later on. Sometimes this signifies studying, investigating, and gathering news—perhaps also the need to keep your ear to the ground.

Twelve

This refers to travel or important visitors from overseas. It can mean a new vehicle or some other new means of transportation, a change of address, or some other change in your immediate environment. New friendships and possibly a new lover can be indicated.

Thirteen

Women will figure strongly in your life soon, either as friends, lovers, at work, in the family, or in any other way. This should be beneficial.

Fourteen

Men will figure strongly in your life soon, either as friends, lovers, at work, in the family, or in any other way. This should be beneficial.

Fifteen

This can mean a completely fresh start, but it can also mean an adjustment or improvement in a current situation.

Sixteen

A partnership matter will prove successful. This can be personal or business.

Seventeen

Success in matters connected to love, but business or career matters will be problematic and this may affect your love life.

Eighteen

This suggests that a wish will come true, so it can refer to just about anything that you may be hoping for.

5

The I Ching

his is usually pronounced *Eee Ching*. This is a Chinese system of divination that dates back in some form to around 8,000 years ago—and it is incredible to consider that this was actually the tail end of the last ice age! The I Ching is known as the "Book of Changes" because the system uses a series of lines that can be read once and then changed for a second reading. There is a method of reading that relies on sticks, and no doubt this predated the invention of coins, but the coin method is the easiest for a Westerner to use.

For the reading, you will need a clean table or one with a clean cloth on it, a pen and some paper, plus three coins of the same type. These can be those imitation Chinese coins that you see in Feng Shui shops or ordinary coins, such as an American quarter or a British ten pence piece. If the coins are not modern ones, choose which side is heads and which is tails, and then designate the heads as Yang and the tails as Yin. Gather the coins into your hands and focus on a question that is on your mind or on the mind of your querent if you are doing this for someone else, and then throw the coins down fairly gently.

If two or more coins land with their heads up, draw a complete (Yang) line on your piece of paper but if two or more coins fall with their tails up, draw a broken (Yin) line on your paper. If it happens that all three coins fall with their heads or tails up, mark the line with a small cross (X), as these will later become your *changing* lines. Do the same thing a second time, drawing your second line above the first, and then repeat the process until you have six lines. This will be your hexagram.

Check the key to the hexagrams in this book and note down the number of your hexagram. If you have marked any lines with a cross, draw up a second hexagram but change the marked lines from Yang to Yin and vice versa. The second hexagram will offer further information and guidance regarding the question. The following illustration is an example of a hexagram where two lines came about as a result of three heads or tails being thrown. Note the "changes" in the second hexagram.

Hexagram 1   **Hexagram 2**

X = changed line =

= changed line =

It is worth noting that the I Ching is far more useful for business, financial, and practical questions than it is for romantic or family ones. This is because in times gone by, Chinese people married for practical reasons rather than romantic ones, and their main concern was for the family and its survival during hard times. However, with a little imagination, you can adapt the answers to fit any situation..

The I Ching readings in this book are very brief, but if you decide that you would like to know more about the I Ching and other Chinese fortune telling methods, please see the books listed in Further Reading.

The 64 Hexagrams of the I Ching

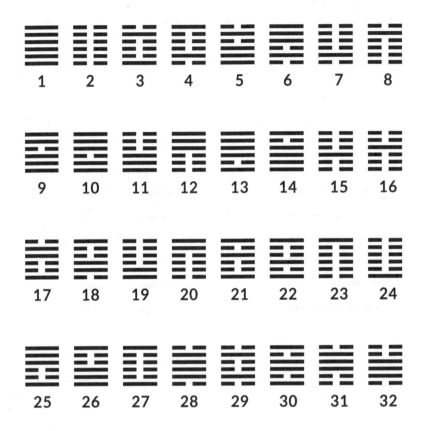

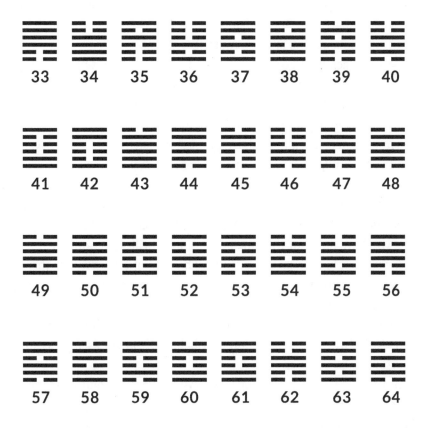

Interpreting the Hexagrams

1. Work hard to gain your objectives but don't overreach yourself.
2. To some extent your future happiness is in the hands of others, so don't rush in and grab at it for yourself.
3. Expect to reach your goals in a slow and steady manner. Other people will give you help and guidance.
4. Take advice and expect to learn slowly. Don't put on airs and graces but be ready to listen to the wisdom of others.
5. There is danger ahead, so don't plunge into anything—rather wait until times are better. When you do begin to make a move forward, there will be friends around who will help you.
6. Although you are probably in the right, this is not a good time to argue or to state your point. Accept criticism, even a lack of credit for work that you have done for the time being. Things will soon improve.
7. You will soon have to face some kind of battle, but others will be there to help you. Whether you fight or retreat is for you to decide, but you will receive guidance.
8. Peace and harmony surround you now. Be sincere in all that you do and expect to make some efforts on behalf of others as well as for yourself.
9. Times may be hard for a while, but with a sensible and economic approach you will achieve your aims, then you will appreciate the good things all the more when they arrive. Restraint, sincerity, and regard for others will be needed.
10. Be firm, even with yourself. Tread the straight and narrow path. Don't hesitate; others will take advantage of you and you will lose your stride.
11. Share your happiness and good fortune with others who are less well off. This should be a time to get things done, to plant for the future or to harvest from the past.

12. Move forward slowly and carefully. From small beginnings, you can make gradual growth but be careful to do this in a modest manner. Doors will soon open for you.

13. There is light at the end of the tunnel. You will soon be able to make better progress and pass from obscurity into a brighter and more successful future. Success will be yours, but you should share the benefits of this with others in order to help them.

14. Work and study will go together. By learning or training, you will be in a better position to understand how to tackle the tasks ahead of you. Don't go overboard in trying to impress others, just grasp the basics and work at the job quietly.

15. Be modest—this will encourage others to help you rather than to stand in your way. Others will admire you for your progress as long as you don't push it down their throats.

16. You will need to advertise both yourself and your wares and to create an enthusiastic atmosphere. Avoid arrogance or self-satisfaction as this will put others off your ideas, and don't fall for your own propaganda.

17. This is a time to drift with the current and to let others show you the way or take the initiative on your behalf. You will be in charge of your own affairs again soon enough.

18. You will soon have to put something right, and you may have to apologize or sort out some kind of misunderstanding. Be scrupulously honest in all your dealings now and be *seen* to be in the right.

19. In the recent past it was right for you to assert yourself in order to get where you are now, but now is the time to be magnanimous. Be cautious and advance slowly forward. Be generous to others.

20. You will need to keep your eyes open with regard to practical matters, and also to contemplate wider philosophical issues. Don't take things on trust, but be penetrative and intuitive.

21. Be careful to stress any positive achievements that you have made however small they may be. Don't allow others to stress the negative or unsuccessful aspects of your life. Don't allow petty jealousy in others to get you down.

22. Dress well and look successful in order to sell an idea to others to give an appearance of success, but, once you have accomplished your aim, don't continue to live life beyond your means. Contemplation and solitude will be necessary to bring equilibrium soon.

23. The odds are against you now. Some aspect of your life will be destroyed so that you can build afresh for the future. Guard against allowing a situation to develop where people who are close to you undermine you from the inside.

24. Attune yourself to nature and to the seasons and develop a sense of timing. A change of seasons will bring improvements and a renewal of energy. Be patient.

25. Don't rush in where angels fear to tread. Be honest and stay within your own limitations. Heaven will guide you. Be unselfish and simple and don't allow temporary setbacks to upset you.

26. You will make great advances in your career but probably not just yet. Work hard and progress slowly, for success is on the way to you.

27. This symbol stands for watchful waiting. This is not a time for accomplishment, so the querent should take the opportunity to rest and build up his mental and physical strength for future times of action.

28. A heavy branch breaks when it is overloaded; therefore the querent shouldn't take on too much at this time. It is better to know one's limitations and to work within them.

29. There are pitfalls ahead and any decisions taken now would place you in a worse position than you are presently in. You should wait for better times to come along before taking action.

30. Intellectual pursuits will go well. An intellectual and logical approach to life would be helpful now.

31. Don't envy those who seem to be cleverer or more successful than you are. Remember, the bigger they are, the harder they fall.

32. Stay put, persevere, and allow things to take their course. Haste will bring problems. Don't insist on having things all your own way, because a casual attitude would be far better. Wait, be yourself, and you will get all that you want.

33. There are crafty people around you who will seek to take advantage. Watch out for traps and don't fall into them. However, you will have to use some guile yourself in order to slide out of any tricky situations.

34. If you have to use strong words, back them up with meaningful action or no one will take you seriously and you will be seen as an empty blusterer.

35. Your situation is improving rapidly and your fortunes are on the way up. Be honest in all your dealings and also be open so that jealous people will not be able to point fingers at you later.

36. When depression and hard times arrive, be cautious and restrained but don't allow yourself to be ground down by misery. Wait: things *will* improve. Just do what you have to do and refrain from moaning to others about your troubles.

37. Attend to your normal daily duties and make your present surroundings comfortable and your present situation happier. Deal with problems right away rather than trying to escape from them. The accent will be on family life where you will have to be fair but also tolerant.

38. Don't insist that you are right, be flexible and allow some leeway to others. Even if you know that you are right, don't ram the fact down the throats of others.

39. If you have a problem, try to go around it rather than to moan about it. Alternatively, you can go out on a limb to solve it. Get help from others

and also help others yourself where you can, because one day you may be facing the same problems that they have.

40. An acute situation may come to a head now, after which you will at least know where you stand. Free yourself from unnecessary encumbrances so that you are in a position to move forward confidently.

41. If others help you to prosper, don't keep all the proceeds to yourself. Redistribute some of the goodies so that everyone benefits.

42. Make the most of any opportunity that comes your way but realize that a good deal of your success will be due to luck rather than your own cleverness. It is worth bearing in mind that at times like these, even an incompetent idiot can succeed.

43. Some form of insurance may be necessary now, as even the best placed of people can run into trouble. Don't allow evil to destroy the things that have been good up to now.

44. Don't be influenced by others, especially if they are stronger than you. Calm persuasion will help you influence other people both near and far.

45. Opposition will face you soon. Don't tackle this head on or make yourself unpopular by opening your mouth too much. Go with the crowd, or, if that is not possible, find one good ally and stick to him.

46. Progress slowly and steadily now. Don't give up—just move steadily onward and upward.

47. There will be hard times soon. Don't run away from them but look within yourself and find the strength to cope with them. Adversity can sometimes be a good thing as it brings out abilities that you never thought you had. Have confidence, don't beat your head against the wall, stay calm, and cope as well as you can.

48. Work will be monotonous but it has to be done. Share any benefits that you have accrued with others but watch that they don't take the credit for your efforts or place difficulties in your way.

49. Your outer manner and presentation will improve and you will soon begin to look more impressive to others.

50. Whatever you are doing, take care to ensure that your tools, equipment, and vehicles are working properly. Don't worry about small mishaps but guard against major ones.

51. There will be stormy weather ahead. Don't panic, just wait until it passes and then reassess your situation.

52. Take things easily and progress slowly along your present path. Don't try to take any unnecessary gambles or any more difficult jobs than you are already coping with.

53. Develop slowly. Your progress may be imperceptible to others but it exists nonetheless.

54. If you cannot get what you want, want what you can get. If you demand too much you could find yourself overburdened with responsibilities, whereas if you do well in what you are engaged upon right now, you will be appreciated all the more. More opportunities will shortly come your way.

55. You will be inwardly happy and troubles on the outside will not be able to harm you and they will soon pass away.

56. You may have to travel soon or have to sell yourself in some way to others, perhaps by going out to get a new job. Look to your manner and your appearance and be careful with whom you associate at this time.

57. Be reasonable and others will accept your ideas. Bend with the wind and go along with the majority opinion for the time being.

58. Inner contentment will be reflected outwardly to others and outer harmony will generate inner peace. In other words, a strong spiritual center will be reflected back by others.

59. Don't be inflexible or allow your opinions to harden. On the other hand, don't allow them to dissolve into nothing either. Be reasonable.

60. You will need to be cautious and to accept certain limitations soon. Reserves of energy, goods, or money will be needed while you sit out a difficult situation. When doors are once again open to you, you will be able to move through them. In the meantime, go by the rules, even if they are someone else's.

61. Watch out for warning signs, there will be stormy weather ahead.

62. Don't lose your way when storms arrive but make for a safe perch. Don't waste your energy or get upset needlessly.

63. You have gone through considerable troubles to get where you are now, so don't lose all that you have gained through stupid actions. Try not to look backward too much, because your circumstances are changing and you will soon be able to be more optimistic. Work to consolidate what you have achieved so far in order to build for the future.

64. Move forward cautiously, keeping your eyes and ears open. Experience will count for much now. Wait for the right moment to make your move; then do so with care and caution.

6

The Runes

Seldiy Bate and Nigel Bourne are well known and well respected members of the British psychic and spiritual scene. They can be seen at psychic festivals, they hold workshops on a variety of subjects, and they also write for a number of magazines. Seldiy gave me the benefit of her experience as a Rune reader, which helped to bring this chapter to life. Nigel helped us out by adding information and also pouring us all a glass or two of wine.

Ritual and invocation

The best Runes are always those that you make for yourself. It is traditional before beginning this to make a dedication to the Norse god Odin, who discovered them. Legend tells us that Odin hung himself upside down from the sacred tree Yggdrasil, and he stayed like this for nine days, during which he reached a stage of enlightenment, and then found the Runes among the roots of the tree. Odin is the Norse equivalent of the Roman god Mercury and the Greek god Hermes or the Egyptian god Thoth. In other words, he is associated with communication, intellect, logic, travel, and healing. However, Odin is also particularly associated with divination.

You can begin by burning some incense, which is sacred to Odin, such as mastic gum or tiny strips of hazelwood. Make an invocation to Odin and visualize the god himself while speaking aloud. He has only one eye and hides the empty socket under the brim of a large hat. He also wears a cloak, carries a blackthorn staff, and is accompanied by a raven. He rides the magical, eight-legged horse, Sleipnir.

Invocation to Odin

Lord of the Northern Wind, by Sea and Sky,
By Baldur's burning Sun and Freya's Moon,
I call upon thee, O Mighty Odin, that I
May learn the secret of each and every Rune!
I have worked the Magicks well and poured
A libation of mead by the trembling blackthorn tree,
Have listened to the Raven's voice and scored
My name upon a hazel wand for thee;
For he that calls the Divine King Odin and proves
Himself to be worthy of the wisdom will hear
The eightfold drumming of Sleipnir's flashing hooves
And know the wisest of the Gods is near.
A gift demands a gift, Grim Guardian of Death
Whisper'd secrets on Odin's sacred breath!

(Seldiy Bate, Summer Solstice, 1987)

To make the Runes

Ideally, these should be made of wood. Hazel wood is traditional, but any type of wood that you like will do (except yew, the tree of Death). If you take a branch from a living tree, don't forget to ask the tree for its permission first. Be careful to select a branch that will not damage the tree irrevocably and place a silver coin somewhere in the tree for payment. Leave the wood a while to season. Slivers of wood can be used or you can cut the branch into slices like a loaf of bread. You will need to make twenty-five

Runes, but it is a good idea to cut more than this number so that you have some to spare of you make a mistake in the lettering.

If you practice magic, cut the letters into the Runes with your own personal magical knife, otherwise cut the letters with any good sharp knife or burn them in with a pokerwork needle which you can buy from a craft shop. If you can cope with the idea, you may place a little blood on at least one of the Runes, so prick your thumb with a clean needle. You can mark each Rune with a tiny dot at one end to show which would be upright if you wish to use upright and reversed readings. Darken the engravings on the Runes with red ink (to represent blood), or a mixture of soot and water or maybe some mead which is sacred to Odin.

Runes can also be made from slivers of bone or soft stone such as limestone. Pebbles of equal size can be used and they look very nice if the design is carefully painted on and then the whole stone is varnished. Any modeling clay that you can buy in a craft shop can be used. This may be the type that you need to fire or the kind that hardens by itself. Failing all this, buy yourself a set of Runes that you feel drawn to. However you come by your Runes, you will need to consecrate them. They should be washed in natural running water (or a token of spring water dabbed on the back of each Rune). You should then waft them through some appropriate incense and make a prayer.

Make yourself a bag for your Runes. This can be leather, felt, or silk—ideally anything that can be pulled closed with a drawstring. Finally, you should make a Rune wand from a hazel twig or a piece of dowel. This should fit into the Rune bag along with your Runes. You can mark the wand with the Runic symbols for your initials, and then paint, decorate, or varnish it.

Casting the Runes

The simplest method is to ask your querent to dip into the Rune bag and pick out whatever number of Runes you need to work with. Alternatively, lay all the Runes out face downward, ask the querent to swirl them around on the table (or Rune cloth, if used) and then to pick out whatever number you require. He should then hold his chosen Runes in his hands for a few moments while thinking about his life. The Runes can be used for a general reading or to answer a specific question.

Layouts

A clock shape can be used with each Rune representing one month of the year. The clock shape can also represent the astrological houses. Astrology is not a Norse divination but many professional readers find this convenient because they are familiar with it. Another simple idea is to draw two large circles, the inner one representing the immediate future and the outer one showing more distant events. The inner circle can indicate people and situations that are close to the querent, while the outer one symbolizes the outside environment of work, strangers, and distant situations. A square divided into four could show various areas of life such as the family, work, health, and relationships. Indeed, a whole roulette table of sections could be worked out. However, a few basic divisions will help, especially when the querent is a stranger to you, in which case you don't automatically know what is on his mind.

The Futhork Alphabet and Its Symbolism

There is some variation in Runic alphabets—this one is sometimes called the Futhork alphabet after its first six letters.

FEOH
English equivalent: F
Keyword :   Cattle

Cattle represented prosperity or wealth in the ancient world, much as they do in parts of Africa today. So this Rune represents the querent's personal property and funds, his wealth, and also status and position—also his career (or lack of one), in terms of material security, and sometimes also emotional security. This Rune represents the fulfillment of love, and if appropriate, of pregnancy, as well as fertility and growth of all kinds.

Inverted meaning

Financial loss and a lack of fulfillment. Sexual frustration, difficulties related to procreation. Female health problems, also problems related to weight gain.

UR
English equivalent: U or W
Keyword: Wild ox

The wild ox was considered a symbol of great physical strength. It represents masculinity, the active principle and also the physical and material planes. This brings opportunities to better oneself, possibly also a financial improvement, but always with the expenditure of energy or strength. This sometimes denotes the acquisition and controlled use of a physical skill or the training of such in others.

Inverted meaning

Missed opportunities. Lack of strength. This may be physical or metaphorical weakness, alternatively perhaps misplaced power or uncontrolled strength.

THORN

English equivalent:	TH
Keyword:	A thorn

The thorn protects the plants from predators; therefore this represents protection in all its forms, be they physical, mental, or even psychic. This may mean protection from attack, physical defenses, and even the use of an offensive deterrent if other Runes nearby indicate this. This can also mean using verbal defense or protecting others. If there are decisions to be taken, they will require a certain element of caution and self-protection. The querent must allow matters to run their course and not force anything. This Rune can also indicate family matters.

Inverted meaning

Making a bad decision. Aggression used for the wrong reasons, perhaps a misplaced use of power, jealousy, or an over-defensive attitude. Also, tension and introversion.

OS

English equivalent:	A or O
Keyword:	A god

This Rune is sacred to Odin so can be used in any invocation to him, as Odin is the chief of the gods of Magic. This Rune represents authority, superiors, elders, and ancestors. Parents and all that can be inherited from them are indicated, as is any kind of father figure or god figure in the querent's life. This can also apply to the querent's spiritual progress, beliefs, and philosophy, and it can denote guidance from above.

Inverted meaning

Problems related to parents or authority figures, even government bodies of some kind. An over-dominant attitude and abuse of power. Also blind faith, fanaticism, obsession, and complexes.

RAD

English equivalent:	R
Keyword:	A wheel

This Rune represents movement; therefore it could suggest a journey with a purpose. This includes transport matters and all kinds of physical movement and exploration but also mental travel, such as studying and using one's imagination. There may be movement in the querent's affairs shortly, especially if there is something that he has neglected or left on the back burner for a while. This Rune relates to changes, the turning of events, and progress forward.

Inverted meaning

Difficulties related to travel and transport. Perhaps a journey that is necessary but not enjoyable such as a visit to a sick person or to see someone who is in a position of authority. This may indicate immobility or stubbornness and a lack of imagination or changes for the sake of change that do nothing to enhance the querent's life.

KEN

English equivalent: K or a hard C
Keyword: A bonfire

This Rune brings warmth and light into the querent's life and traditional celebrations—possibly around a bonfire or a barbecue. The querent will be the center of attention and there will be pleasant social gatherings. It can also suggest mental illumination or a burst of creative energy. This Rune is especially lucky for a woman, as she can expect to receive love from a man, whilst a male querent would find himself in the position of giving love. This may indicate the kindling of a new relationship. There is also a feeling of status and success and it may also signify an improvement in health or a period of healing.

Inverted meaning

The querent's life may lack warmth and there may also be a lack of direction and guidance—possibly a feeling of blindness. There may be the loss of something that is valuable. There may be health problems, especially heart trouble or a general lowering of resistance.

GYFU

English equivalent: G
Keyword: A gift

This Rune may bring a gift, a contract, or an opportunity. It suggests that the querent has some kind of useful gift or talent. This also brings beneficial partnerships and happiness in love but it implies that "give and take" must be part of the relationship. In Runic lore, we are never given anything for nothing, so we must be prepared to pay in some way for whatever we receive.

Inverted meaning

There may be a loss or even a swindle now. The querent may find that he lacks the necessary talent or qualities for a particular job that he would like to do. This Rune can also suggest a sacrifice, and when inverted it betokens a pointless one such as martyrdom or exploitation; it also can imply an illness or some shortcoming that the querent has to accept.

WYN

English equivalent:	W or U
Keyword:	Joy

This Rune brings joy and happiness on an emotional level. It is associated with water, and therefore it suggests a journey over water or perhaps a home near water. Alternatively, an important visitor could come from over the water. There may be an artistic or spiritual awakening and there may also be gain or luck in respect of creative or inspirational matters. Sometimes this Rune foretells the appearance of a fair-haired man.

Inverted meaning

Over-emotion, martyrdom, and depression. The querent is advised to avoid making major decisions as he is probably too emotionally involved with the problem at hand. There is difficulty in seeing clearly and also bad judgement. This Rune suggests the need to wait three months before making a decision that is directly related to an emotional matter or three days before making a decision related to work. There may be problems concerning the digestive system or with the body fluids, or in the case of a female, with the menstrual cycle or the hormone balance.

HAGAL

English equivalent: H

Keyword: Hail

This represents a bolt from the blue that may result from some kind of natural disaster or some unexpected twist of fate. This Rune implies havoc, disruption of plans, and unforeseen events. Even good events are possible, but they might turn the querent's world upside down. There may be sickness in the family or unexpected pregnancies. The querent must be prepared for the unexpected, but if there is destruction, this allows him to rebuild in a better way. It is even possible that the disaster is self-inflicted or deserved in some way. Sometimes this Rune warns of a death but only if other Runes that are near it emphasize this possibility. It is not worth giving an inverted meaning to Hagal as it means much the same either way up.

NYD

English equivalent: N

Keyword: Need

Associated with necessity, self-preservation, and natural instincts, such as the need for food, shelter, and to protect oneself and one's children. This Rune also rules such needs as creativity, the need for a job, or a relationship. The motivating force is the need to function and to achieve. There is also a warning here to be patient and to exercise restraint.

Inverted meaning

This seems to imply physical tension and emotional tightness. This may belong to the kind of cautious, greedy, envious personality who is hard to get along with. There is an inability to let go and feelings that are bottled up. This can lead to mental problems; sickness, muscular strain, and all kinds of stress related factors.

IS

English equivalent: I

Keyword: Ice

There is an impediment, an obstacle, and a feeling that everything is frozen up. Plans may be halted, money may be immobilized, and nothing good can come of the present situation, so the instruction here is to leave things alone and to try again another time. Feelings might be frozen and there may be too much detachment for the querent. This is like the ice of winter that always melts in the spring, so there will be a time of warmth and growth but patience is needed.

Inverted meaning

The same but worse! There may be fear, coldness, and avoidance. There could be some physical impediment such as rheumatism or paralysis. Perhaps there is immobility or mental paralysis with no clear or constructive ideas, in addition to obstinacy and a refusal to adapt.

GER or YER

English equivalent: Y or soft G

Keyword: Cycle or harvest

The end of a cycle is in sight, and this is like the turning of the seasons or the wheel of fortune. There may be a waiting period, a time of expectation, and a promise of fulfillment. The querent will reap what has been sown for good or for ill. This time of change is inevitable and it should be used constructively. This is a time to pay debts, to make a start on new projects, sign contracts, and perhaps even to move. In other words, this is the time for a fresh start.

Inverted meaning

This Rune is really much the same either way up, but opportunities may be missed as a result of the querent's resistance to change or an inability to see the advantages of a situation. A cycle, or indeed a waiting period of a year, is indicated.

EOH

English equivalent:	E (as in egg)
Keyword:	Yew bow

The yew bow is flexible enough to adapt itself to a new shape without breaking; therefore this suggests a kind of recoiling, retreating, or stepping out of the way of difficulty. The querent will have to take a flexible approach to life and adapt himself to a new and different situation. He may even take one step backward in order to move two steps forward. Pitfalls will be avoided, and inconvenient situations will turn out advantageous in the end. The querent may be able to use the strength of others against them (as in Judo), or to avoid the manipulative behavior of others or their dominance in order to find another way around a problem. He will need to do some lateral thinking.

Inverted meaning

There may be indecision, vacillation, and a retrograde step in one's progress. There may be withdrawal, even a relapse, into physical or mental sickness. There may be deviousness and craftiness, refusal to face up to problems, or escapism.

PEORTH

English equivalent: P

Keyword: The secret Rune

Something is not being revealed to the querent and he will receive the knowledge or information only at the right time. If this is the first Rune to appear in a reading, it might be better to leave it and try again a few days or even a few weeks later. This suggests a link with the spirit world, psychism, dreams, visions, and trance-like states which may bring forth prophecy. Also unexpectedly good events, luck, abundance, the return of favors that the querent may have forgotten. Unexpected benefit.

Inverted meaning

Imaginary fears, disappointments. Favors that are not returned. Lack of communication or going behind someone's back. This Rune can also indicate subconscious fears, phobias, and deeply hidden psychoses.

EOLHS

English equivalent: E or Y

Keyword: A hand held upright in greeting. A reed

The reed definition of this Rune has connections with the reed in a musical instrument, in that it suggests artistry, poetry, and creative talent or self-expression. This denotes hobbies, cultural interests, and study for pleasure. The greeting definition signifies belonging to a special group that uses its own behavior and vocabulary.

Inverted meaning

There are people who the querent should avoid: groups who behave stupidly or illegally or who are a bad influence. Can also denote a lack of creativity, self-expression, or the lack of opportunity for self-expression.

SYGEL

English equivalent:	S
Keyword:	The sun

The sun was viewed as the source of life in the ancient world, and in a way, it still is now. Therefore, this Rune represents the life force, health and healing, and also rest and recuperation. It rules relaxation and activities such as sport, hobbies, vacations, and entertainment. On other levels, it can indicate success, fame, recognition, and bringing a creative endeavor or talent out into the light.

Inverted meaning

This is the same as the upright meaning.

TIR or TYR

English equivalent:	T
Keyword:	Tir, the war god

Tir is the Norse god of war (similar to Mars); therefore this Rune implies activity, energy, and heroism. If the querent is male, he will seek romance soon, and if female, there will soon be a new lover or partner. Any ensuing romance would be high-octane, full of passion and overwhelming feelings. There may also be anger, aggression, angst, and attack.

Inverted meaning

Lack of energy or something that is misdirected. For a male querent, a broken love affair or unrequited love, possibly caused by being too pushy. For a female, possibly falling for the wrong person or an obsessive relationship. Other possibilities are sexual frustration, impotence, arguments, damage to property, violence, cuts, burns, bruises, accidents, headaches, or allergies.

BEORC

English equivalent:	B
Keyword:	Birch tree

The birch is associated with fertility cults and pagan ritual, particularly that which is concerned with spring and the awakening of the life force. Therefore, this Rune can mean new beginnings, expansion, celebrations, weddings, and births. It represents joy in the family but also ritual, familiarity, and repetition or routine.

Inverted meaning

A plan that doesn't come to fruition, barrenness, and delays. It can indicate sickness in the family, disconcerting visits, unfamiliar surroundings, bad news, or ill will in the community. Also, fatigue and a lack of energy.

EOW

English equivalent:	E as in egg
Keyword:	Horse

This relates to travel and transport, movement, and methods of transport such as the querent's car, the bus that he takes, or even his feet. On a working farm, this relates to animals, but it can also signify pets. This Rune is concerned with change and the methods that are used to bring it about, in addition to ideas and the medium that is used to put them across to others. This is related to all forms of communication and progress, and how it is achieved.

Inverted meaning

Problems with transport and delays. Sick animals feature here, as do sick people, immobility, and handicaps. Also, failure to get a message across or the wrong approach.

MAN

English equivalent:	M
Keyword:	Man

This Rune represents a male figure, a man in authority, or a professional man. The Rune tells the querent not to forge ahead with any project without consulting a professional person. This person may be a doctor, lawyer, accountant, or even a plumber, a computer buff, or some other form of craftsman, as appropriate. The querent should delay making decisions until after all such consultations have taken place.

Inverted meaning

This may indicate problems related to authority figures such as the police, judiciary, or the querent's boss. There may be abuse of power or position, or there may be an influential person who stands for something different to the querent. Perhaps there is a domineering father figure around or maybe a foreigner or someone from an alien environment. If this is a true enemy, look at the surrounding Runes for more information.

LAGU

English equivalent:	L
Keyword:	Lake

This is a feminine Rune that is connected to the moon goddess, the sea, the psychic realms, intuition, and the mysteries of childbirth. This symbolizes anything that allows change, fluidity and conduction, and any kind of medium. It also applies to protection and a kind of womb-like safety. It can indicate a woman in a reading—although she has to be of an age and type who is capable of giving birth. Thus, also fertility and children. This rules the unknown and the universal world of the spirit rather than personal affairs.

Inverted meaning

Paranoia and the inability to cope with the subconscious. Blood, menstrual problems, or other cyclic problems. Hormone imbalances, miscarriage, and infertility. Also escapism, alcoholism, and drug dependence. If the querent is overemotional or too emotionally involved with a problem, he should consult someone impartial.

ING

English equivalent:	NG
Keyword:	The Danes. The family Rune

This represents fertility, production, and material results, also the earth, fruition, and children. The idea is that something produces a result or completes a project, and this can apply to long term projects or problem solving. It also suggests protection; enclosure, security, and staying put in familiar surroundings. If a realistic effort is put into problem solving, at the end of the relevant cycle, they will be solved. This Rune can refer to friends—particularly if they are from overseas. It is also associated with magic, divination, and women's mysteries by an association with the mother goddess.

Inverted meaning

There may be a lack of productiveness, a lack of charity or tolerance, and perhaps also imprisonment, restriction, and tension. This Rune can indicate health problems related to tension, stress and blockages, claustrophobia, and infertility.

ETHEL

English equivalent:	E or O
Keyword:	Inheritance

This denotes benefit through property, gifts, and help from older relatives, also inheritance, heirlooms, and an actual object that is left to the querent. It is also associated with documents, wills, legal matters, and anything related to money.

Inverted meaning

The querent may be bound by old conditioning and he may refuse to let go of outmoded ideas and concepts. Sometimes this denotes overturning the established order of things and bringing chaos to the family or group. Perhaps the querent needs to consider what benefits you and others.

DAEG

English equivalent:	D
Keyword:	Day

This signifies daytime, warmth, and light, so it refers to anything that is open, obvious, and easily seen. This represents things that come to light and also face values. It can indicate advertisement, image, clarity, and recognition. Also success in studies, passing tests and gaining qualifications, a change for the better, and success in general. If this is close to the blank Rune, the success is a matter of fate or destiny. It may be worth setting an appropriate date for something to happen, making relevant preparations and then waiting for it to come around.

Inverted meaning

This Rune means much the same either way up but occasionally it can refer to sunset or the ending of a phase in one's life. It can mean sleep, illness, or even coma, also things that are hidden and answers that are not immediately obvious.

The Blank Rune
Keyword: Destiny, fate

Traditionalists don't use a blank Rune but it has become common for modern readers to do so. This Rune is associated with fate or anything else that is out of the querent's own hands. This represents those things that are known only to the gods. Look at the Runes that are nearby to see what the fates have in store or use this in some kind of placement system where the destiny becomes clear by the position of the Rune.

Words of warning

Seldiy and Nigel tell us that things can go wrong in the following situations. If you ask a frivolous question, you will be given a frivolous answer. If you become big-headed before you have gained the requisite skills, you will find the skill being taken away from you. Be prepared to study and work hard. By all means practice readings with obliging friends but always accept some payment, no matter how small or in what form. Remember the words of Odin, "A gift demands a gift." Runic lore states that nobody gets anything without some form of payment—even if it is not an obvious one.

7

Dominoes

Tradition states that dominoes should be consulted only on rare occasions; for example, no more than once a month and *never* on a Monday or a Friday.

The method

Place all the dominoes face downward and stir them around. Select only three or four dominoes for your reading. There are several meanings attributed to each domino, so each meaning should be applied to the querent's situation at the time of the reading.

Domino Meanings

Double six

This is a very lucky combination that denotes happiness in relationships and luck in a career or in business, and this is also a good omen for anybody who wants a child. Land and property matters are well-starred, while parents will be caring and helpful.

Six/Five

If the querent is out of work, there will be a new job soon. There is luck in connection with work and relationships but they will need to be worked at. There may be trouble involving children.

Six/Four

Early marriage with children following soon after. A happy life with reasonable security. The querent will need to be careful regarding legal matters.

Six/Three

Marriage to a reliable person and stability in relationships. Illness in middle age. A journey that is successful and good news regarding vehicles.

Six/Two

Love affairs will go well and marriage could be in the air. The partner will be hard working and sensible with money. If the querent is involved in any messy business deals, these will go wrong. A useful gift.

Six/One

Two marriages, the second being the happier. Happiness in middle age. Children will travel and do well. A problem is solved.

Six/Blank

News of a death—this may be animal or human. There is a possibility of jealousy and gossip now and accidents are also possible.

Five/Five

Luck, money, a good career, and a happy marriage. A move that is lucky. Also improvements in health.

Five/Four

Money worries that are associated with some kind of partner. Work will bring money and independence.

Five/Three

Luck in money matters. The querent will never be short of money. Average happiness in relationships. A nice visitor.

Five/Two

Problems in relationships—perhaps unrequited love. A marriage that is made for financial reasons but which lacks warmth. There could be news of the birth of a child or new enterprises.

Five/One

Parties and social events. A love affair with a charismatic person, but this will not last. Money problems may continue.

Five/Blank

A warning against speculative ventures, also against rushing into marriage. A friend may need the querent's shoulder to cry on soon.

Four/Four

Parties and social events, sports and the presence of young people around. Manual work will go well but professional people will experience difficulties.

Four/Three

Disappointments, especially concerning children. Illness is possible, as are problems in connection with a vehicle.

Four/Two

Family and domestic upheavals. Unexpected events concerning the home—these could be good or bad. Beware of flirtations or philandering types of people.

Four/One

A good marriage with comfort and security but possibly without children. The querent will have to pay some outstanding bills soon.

Four/Blank

There will be trouble in connection with relationships, and any reconciliation will be only temporary. There is a possibility of twins coming into the family. A new outlook or a different way of life.

Three/Three

Money will come to the querent soon, possibly via a legacy, a win or a bonus. The querent's love life may go through a bad patch due to outside interference.

Three/Two

This is a good omen for the start of an enterprise. A journey will be enjoyable and worthwhile. Dishonesty will be found out and the querent should not take any chances now.

Three/One

A surprise and good news. The querent may become involved in an affair that lands him in hot water.

Three/Blank

Jealousy, broken friendships. Domestic problems due to the weak attitude of the partner or of other family members.

Two/Two

All partnerships and relationships will go well, but health needs to be watched.

Two/One

Loss or failure in business, and if the querent isn't careful, he could lose his home as well. A flamboyant but unsettled love life.

Two/Blank

Journeys will have a good outcome. Sales and communication ventures will go well. The querent must beware of thieves. Relationship matters are not good just now.

One/One

Love, money, and luck, also happy family life. Parents will be helpful. A decision will be needed soon, but this will require courage.

One/Blank

A visitor comes from over water. Money or resources are in danger of being wasted. Health improves.

Blank/Blank

Loss, theft, disappointment. Troubles are on the way and this could affect the querent's job, relationships, health, or all three. The querent should also try to guard against accidents.

8

Playing Cards

Playing cards are a relatively recent invention that first came into being in France in the 17th century. They are a spin-off from the Minor Arcana of the Tarot deck and also from chess, which itself is a spin-off from the Tarot. A playing card deck comprises fifty-two cards that are arranged in four suits. These suits are similar to those found in the Tarot, but with the Jack replacing both the Page and Knight, and the Joker standing in for the Fool in the Tarot, and indeed for all twenty-two cards of the Major Arcana. The huge popularity of the Tarot is a relatively recent phenomenon; up to the 1970s most skilled card readers used playing cards.

Tarot cards will be considered only as an overview in chapter 18 because there are so many excellent books devoted to it. If you wish to learn the read the Tarot for yourself, several excellent recommendations will be found in the further reading section on page 185.

Playing card links

The four suits in a deck of playing card suits can be linked to those of the Tarot and also to the four elements.

Playing card	Tarot card	Element
Clubs	Wands	Fire
Diamonds	Coins	Earth
Spades	Swords	Air
Hearts	Cups	Water

A new deck

Buy yourself a new deck of cards, keep them in a box away from other people, and use them solely for fortune telling. If you care to make a prayer over the cards before using them for the first time, please do so. It is a good idea to bless the cards and to ask for guidance so that you use them well. Ask for them to bring comfort, help, and good advice to your querent. If you like incense you can use a joss stick while performing this blessing ritual. Shuffle the cards thoroughly several times to remove their newness and to help them tune into your aura and vibrations.

Fortune telling spreads

There are many layouts that can be used, including any that you find in a book on the Tarot or even the Runes. A Romany fortune-teller named Sally showed me the following spread:

Ask your querent to shuffle the cards and then spread them out in a rough line face-downward on the table. Ask him to select fifteen cards and to place them in a rough arrangement face-up on the table. Ask him to spread them out a little, keeping them in the same rough area so that you can see which cards touch each other or which are close to each other. The cards that are close to each other link together in some way. After giving the initial reading, go through the whole process again using twenty-one cards and see what develops from the first reading. It is always interesting to note which cards turn up in both spreads.

Other spreads might be a horseshoe, a cross, or three lines of three cards, with one line representing the past, the second indicating the present, and the final showing the past. Frankly, any spread that makes you happy is fine.

In my experience, playing cards are always read in the upright position, but tradition assigns several of the cards a reversed meaning. If you wish to use these meanings, you will need to mark the cards so that you know when they are reversed.

Meanings of the Cards

Some card readers use only thirty-two cards, omitting the lower numbered cards altogether, but the following list includes all fifty-two cards. There are many different forms of interpretations in use, but the following list is probably familiar to card readers. If you discover other interpretations that suit you better, please feel free to use them.

Ace of Hearts

Joy, love, friendship, or the start of a romance.

Reversed
Friendship rather than romance, possibly the end of a love affair.

King of Hearts

Traditionally this represents a fair-haired man who is kind, loving, and affectionate and who will give the querent good advice.

Reversed
Poor judgement. An unreliable philanderer.

Queen of Hearts

Traditionally this signifies a fair-haired woman who is kindly, loving, and good to the querent. She is faithful and affectionate.

Reversed
An over-materialistic attitude. A pleasant but lazy and greedy woman.

Jack of Hearts

Traditionally speaking, this is a fair-haired young man. Look around at the nearby cards to judge his intentions.

Ten of Hearts

Good luck, love, and joy. This card improves any bad cards around it and it confirms the benefits of any good ones.

Nine of Hearts

This is called the "wish card" and it confers health, wealth, status, and esteem. It signifies an improvement in all circumstances.

Eight of Hearts

Visits and visitors, journeys for pleasure, and meals in good company.

Reversed
Irritating visits or visitors.

Seven of Hearts

An unfaithful or unreliable person. Disturbing news.

Six of Hearts

A generous person and perhaps a shoulder to cry upon. Shared confidences, unexpected propositions, and good luck.

Reversed
A friend needs the querent's help.

Five of Hearts

Money coming, but also jealous or unreliable people around.

Four of Hearts

A journey or a change. If applicable, the querent will marry later in life.

Reversed
An irritating journey or an unexpectedly awkward change in circumstances.

Three of Hearts

The querent should exercise caution; rash statements will upset others.

Two of Hearts

Success, happiness, luck, and prosperity. An engagement or even a marriage.

Reversed
The same but delayed.

Ace of Diamonds

An engagement or wedding ring. A letter bringing good news about money.

Reversed
Similar but delayed.

King of Diamonds

Traditionally, a fair- or gray-haired man who is obstinate or powerful but also helpful to the querent.

Reversed
An angry, obstinate man, who will hurt the querent or look for revenge for real or imagined slights.

Queen of Diamonds

Tradition suggests that this is a fair- or gray-haired woman who is flirtatious, sophisticated, and fond of socializing.

Reversed
A very nasty piece of work.

Jack of Diamonds

This is traditionally said to be a fair-haired relative. This person is selfish, dishonest, and only interested in his own requirements and opinions.

Reversed
Avoid this person at all costs.

Ten of Diamonds

Money, journeys, possibly help from a married man who lives in the countryside.

Reversed
Similar but delayed.

Nine of Diamonds

A surprise regarding money. (Good if the card is upright; poor if reversed.)

Eight of Diamonds

A marriage late in life, but this is not necessarily good. Plans and ideas.

Reversed
A bad late marriage.

Seven of Diamonds

A gift or surprise.

Reversed
Waste, the loss of something valuable.

Six of Diamonds

Problems in a marriage, especially if this is a second marriage.

Reversed
The querent shouldn't even contemplate a second marriage.

Five of Diamonds

Success in business or other enterprises. If applicable, good children.

Reversed
Success, but this is delayed.

Four of Diamonds

Inheritance or improvement in finances.

Reversed
Annoyances and irritations.

Three of Diamonds

Legal problems, especially if the querent is involved in a divorce. A bad marriage partner who will make the querent unhappy.

Reversed
Divorce, domestic, and legal problems.

Two of Diamonds

A love affair that meets with opposition.

Reversed
A disappointing love affair.

Ace of Clubs

Wealth, success, and peace of mind, also a happy home life.

Reversed
The same but milder.

King of Clubs

Traditionally a dark-haired man. He is honest, helpful, humane, and affectionate. A faithful partner who makes everyone around him happy.

Reversed
This man may be troubled, in a difficult situation, or just plain tricky and dishonest.

Queen of Clubs

Tradition says that this is a dark-haired woman who is businesslike, capable, and very attractive to the opposite sex.

Reversed

This lady may be worried or not in a position to help the querent. Alternatively, she may be calculating and shifty.

Jack of Clubs

Traditionally a dark-haired young man who is a reliable and helpful friend.

Reversed

A young man either unwilling or unable to help the querent right now.

Ten of Clubs

Money is coming. This might be a bonus, a win, a legacy, a raise, or a business idea that takes off quickly.

Reversed

The same but milder and slower to materialize.

Nine of Clubs

Achievements—and if applicable, a new lover.

Reversed

Obstacles and disagreements.

Eight of Clubs

A greedy, jealous person comes into the querent's life.

Reversed

Opposition, arguments.

Seven of Clubs

Happiness, joy, and prosperity. However, the querent should be careful in dealings with the opposite sex, as they will cause trouble.

Reversed
The same but weaker.

Six of Clubs

Business success, especially in partnerships.

Reversed
The same but milder.

Five of Clubs

An advantageous marriage and helpful friends.

Reversed
Friendship rather than marriage.

Four of Clubs

Changes for the worse, lies, and betrayal.

Reversed
Unreliable people around the querent.

Three of Clubs

Marriage to a wealthy partner.

Reversed
Marriage to a reasonably comfortable (but not rich) partner.

Two of Clubs

Disappointments, disagreements.

Ace of Spades

Love affairs, passion, and obsession. Perhaps, also, deceitful friends.

Reversed

A death around the querent.

King of Spades

Traditionally either a very dark- or fair-haired man who is ambitious. He is a terrific friend but he must guard against losing all that he has.

Reversed

An ambitious, tough, selfish, and aggressive man.

Queen of Spades

Traditionally a very dark- or very fair-haired woman. Tradition also suggests that she is a widow or divorcee. She can be seductive and unscrupulous.

Reversed

A spiteful, jealous woman.

Jack of Spades

This is traditionally a very fair- or very dark-haired young man. He is a well-meaning man who never really gets his act together.

Reversed

Lazy.

Ten of Spades

Worry, imprisonment of any kind. This will cast a cloud over any cards that are nearby.

Reversed

The same but milder.

Nine of Spades

Domestic worries, possibly the total loss of money. Calamity, deaths, natural disasters, destruction, and war.

Reversed
Still terrible but not quite as devastating.

Eight of Spades

Opposition from others, canceled plans, and obstacles.

Reversed
Bad news, opposition, and troubles.

Seven of Spades

Sorrow, warnings, losses, and possibly the death of a friend.

Reversed
Still bad but milder. Tears and sleepless nights.

Six of Spades

Improvements, wage increases, and rewards.

Reversed
No real recognition for work that is done.

Five of Spades

Good marriage, domestic happiness, but bad-tempered people around the querent, albeit outside his home environment.

Reversed
Interference from others, anxiety.

Four of Spades

Illness, business, and money worries.

Three of Spades

A marriage to a wealthy partner who is fickle and unreliable.

Reversed
Possibly a hasty decision. A journey and a parting.

Two of Spades

Scandal, gossip, betrayal.

Reversed
A possible death around the querent, or loss and partings due to interference by others.

Combinations

Playing cards can be read singly or in combination with other cards and there are several approaches to this. The simplest and most effective way is to look at groups of cards that fall close to each other and see if they link together to tell some kind of story. The following chart provides a list of some familiar groupings that are easy to cope with in a reading. This list includes the 32 cards (minus the lower cards) that are traditionally used by most readers.

Basic Combinations

	Four Cards	Three Cards	Two Cards
Aces	Great success and a completely new way of life. The career is especially well-starred.	Success and help to the querent. Good news and luck.	Partnership, possibly a marriage. Unusual news.
Kings	Great success, advancement, inheritance.	Success, important business meetings that will benefit the querent.	Some success, good business partnerships.
Queens	Scandal but also social activity.	Backbiting and nasty remarks coming to the querent. Also invitations.	Some minor gossip. Also an interesting meeting with a female friend.
Jacks	Quarrels. Also noisy parties.	Some quarrelling.	Argument and discussion. Someone has bad intentions toward the querent.
Tens	Change for the better all round.	Money, improvement of circumstances and finances.	Money, a debt repaid.
Nines	Good luck, unexpectedly good events.	Success, most things will go well. Good health, happiness.	Reasonable success. Important documents to deal with.
Eights	Problems, troubles, worry. Short trips to see friends.	Family problems, love troubles. It is best to postpone decisions until better times come along.	Worry. A desire for love but disappointment as this will not come along yet.
Sevens	Several enemies. Disputes, scandal, conspiracies.	Some people seem to be against the querent now. Illness.	One active enemy, but the querent will overcome problems, reach success, and make achievements.

9

Phrenology

Phrenology, or reading the bumps on a person's head, seems like a truly silly idea—but it works! Phrenology is not technically a fortune telling method—one cannot read the future by this method—but understanding phrenology is a way of reading a person's character. After all, if the lines on a person's hands and feet and marks on the eyes can tell a story, why not the bumps on a person's head?

Dr. Gall, a native of Baden in Germany, postulated a connection between the way the mind works and the shape of the cranium, so it was he who developed the concept of phrenology. His idea was that the shape of the head indicates the kind of mind that is contained inside it. He also suggested that a young person's brain could be altered by education and specific kinds of use. This latter statement has proved to be true—and not only for young people, as it is now understood that elderly people's brains keep going if they continue to use them. Unfortunately, phrenology was hijacked by the Nazis (as were many other perfectly reasonable ideas) as a way of showing who was or was not truly "Aryan" and therefore fit to live in Hitler's Third Reich.

The seven major divisions of the head

Victorian phrenologists started by measuring the head to see if it fitted their concept of normality. Any hat maker will tell you that the shape and size of heads vary widely among perfectly normal people. Phrenologists then went on to divide the head into seven spheres, which like so many divinations, they linked to the Sun, Moon, and those planets that were visible with the naked eye.

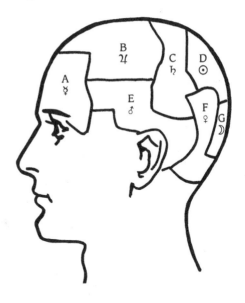

Area A: Associated with the planet Mercury, this is considered to be the seat of the main intellect and the ability to think. This also governs practical things like being able to judge size, distance, people, places, rhythms, and so on.

Area B: Associated with the planet Jupiter, this concerns the things that we find ourselves naturally drawn to, and it rules anything that captures our loyalty and devotion. It seems to affect those things that we are able to appreciate.

Area C: Associated with the planet Saturn, this is concerned with our survival instincts. It rules our urge to protect and safeguard others and ourselves. This seems to rule behavior.

Area D: Associated with the Sun, this governs the whole workings of the mind. It is concerned with our ambitions and the way we set about achieving them. This is concerned with status.

Area E: Associated with the planet Mars, this is concerned with our energies, natural instincts, and appetites. It rules such things as our willingness to fight for what we want and the acquisition of material possessions. This also seems to rule the way that we go about things.

Area F: Associated with the planet Venus, this concerns feelings, affection, love, and sex. This is clearly about personal relationships.

Area G: Associated with the Moon, this concerns our relationship with our family, our home situation, and our place in society. This rules the relationship with the home and family.

The forty-two areas of the head

The seven sections are now subdivided into a total of forty-two sections as per the diagram. I have retained the rather archaic titles of the areas as they were in 19th century texts, but I have modernized the descriptions to make them clear to today's readers.

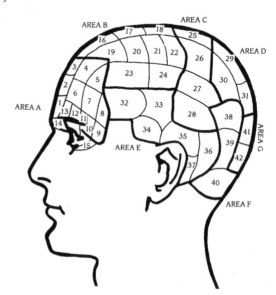

Area A

1. **Individuality**. The power of observation and the ability to discriminate. The larger the bump, the more a person likes dealing with details. If too large, he will be ultra-critical and very inquisitive, but if too small, he will have little curiosity and poor mental faculties.
2. **Eventuality**. A large bump denotes a good memory, while a small one suggests a poor memory and a low level of intellect.
3. **Comparison**. Reasoning ability and powers of analysis. If overlarge, this person will be hypercritical, if too small he will not be able to make comparisons or apply himself to anything.

---

4. **Causality**. This word, so beloved of psychologists, has probably changed its meaning since the 19th century, but in those days it meant powers of deduction. If this area is large, it means that the person has an original mind, good powers of deduction and intuition. It suggests that he would make a good explorer or inventor. If it is small, the mind will be mundane and shallow.

5. **Mirthfulness**. The sense of humor. Obviously a small bump here would suggest that the subject couldn't see a joke.

6. **Locality**. A sense of direction and a memory for places. If large, the subject would have a photographic memory and perhaps also occasional flashes of déjà vu. If small, this suggests that the subject finds visualization difficult and that he lacks a sense of direction.

7. **Time**. A sense of rhythm and timing, also punctuality. A small bump here indicates a lack of rhythm and a tendency to be late for everything.

8. **Tune**. If this bump is developed, the subject has an ear for music.

9. **Calculation**. A large bump here indicates an aptitude for figures.

10. **Order**. If this bump is large, the subject is well-organized and able to work systematically. If it small, he will be disorganized and a messy thinker.

11. **Color**. The ability to judge shades of color and to remember them, also the ability to distinguish distant objects. If large, the subject will be able to use color exceptionally creatively, but if small he may have difficulty in seeing objects at a distance and he may be color blind.

12. **Weight**. This governs the ability to judge the weight of objects, the ability to balance objects on top of each other, or in keeping one's own balance.

13. **Size**. This governs the ability to judge the size of an object or of a room space.

14. **Form**. This relates to the ability to see and remember people and objects. Artistic people have a well-developed bump here. An overlarge

bump can make the subject oversensitive to atmospheres or places, while a small one indicates a person who is oblivious to people and to his surroundings.

15. **Language**. A well-developed bump belongs to a good communicator who has a way with words, and it can indicate an aptitude for foreign languages. If overlarge, the subject will talk too much, while if small he will be reticent, hesitant, or fumbling in his speech.

Area B

16. **Humanity**. Sometimes called the bump of intuition, this gives deep understanding of the motives of others. If underdeveloped, the subject cannot understand others and is indifferent to them.

17. **Benevolence**. If overdeveloped, the subject will be overgenerous toward others; if underdeveloped, he is miserly with both his time and his money.

18. **Veneration**. A respect for values and traditions. If overdeveloped, this might indicate a religious fanatic, but if small, he will hold nothing sacred and he might have a destructive nature.

19. **Agreeableness**. Popularity, charm, and pleasantness. If overlarge, the subject could be effusive or too keen to make himself liked while if small he is hostile and offensive.

20. **Imitativeness**. The ability to learn through imitation. A small bump here might suggest an independent and eccentric manner or a lack of ability to learn by imitation.

21. **Spirituality**. Religious or spiritual feelings. If overlarge, the person will be too otherworldly to cope with daily life. If small, the mind will only be able to cope with things that can be seen, touched, heard, etc.

22. **Hopefulness**. Optimism and forward thinking. Too large a bump denotes a lack of realism while a very small one represents a pessimist.

23. **Ideality**. An appreciation of beauty and the better things for which

man strives. If the bump is overlarge, the subject is unrealistic, but if small he will lack imagination, culture or ideals.

24. **Sublimity**. A love of romance as in romantic scenery, thrilling experiences the wild grandeur of places and appreciation of all that is best in the world. If overlarge, the subject will overdramatize everything, but if small he will have no romance in his soul and he will be a wet blanket.

Area C

25. **Firmness**. This endows the subject with determination and self-discipline but if it is overlarge he will be a tyrant or a despot. If small, the person will be irresponsible and unable to finish anything that he starts. He may be easily led into temptation and easily bullied by stronger people.

26. **Conscientiousness**. If this is overdeveloped, the person will be nervous and neurotic, but if small he will be indifferent to the needs of others and he will lack principle.

27. **Caution**. If overlarge, the subject will be too fearful to achieve anything, but if small he will be reckless.

28. **Secretiveness**. A bump here denotes the ability to keep a confidence. An overlarge bump denotes a crafty person who enjoys plotting against others, while a small one belongs to someone who cannot keep quiet about anything.

Area D

29. **Self-esteem**. This could be the most important attribute of all because without this we can achieve nothing and we lay ourselves open to manipulation by stronger or less principled people. If the bump is very large, the person will be pompous and full of self-aggrandizement, if small he will be self-effacing and easily pushed around.

30. **Approbativeness**. This concerns status and standing in the community and the amount of praise that we attract. It rules politeness and social skills. If the bump is large, the subject may be full of himself. Alternatively, he may be famous, respected, or an authority on a particular subject. If small, he will be indifferent to the opinions of others and perhaps also antisocial.

31. **Continuity**. Concentration and mental application. If the bump is overlarge, the subject could be obsessive, but if it is small, he won't be able to concentrate on anything for long.

Area E

32. **Constructiveness**. This is the bump of the maker and doer, the do-it-yourself expert, or the creative dressmaker, cook, or artist. A large bump here could indicate a person who is always busily engaged with some project or other. A small one denotes a lack of dexterity and a lack of interest in making anything.

33. **Acquisitiveness**. The ability to earn money, to collect goods, and also to obtain knowledge. Obviously, if this is overlarge, the subject will be a miser and hoarder, and he may lack honesty due to an intense desire to amass things. A small bump denotes a drifter or perhaps someone whose values are not materialistic.

34. **Alimentiveness**. This bump is concerned with the connection between the brain, the sense of taste, and the stomach. It regulates the desire to eat and drink. If it is overlarge, the subject will be a glutton and a drunkard. If it is very small, he will not be interested in eating and drinking. To quote an ancient book, "fakirs and other hermits who considered starvation to be necessary to their spiritual well-being have very small bumps of alimentiveness." This seems to indicate that eating and drinking is less due to mind over matter than to one's nature!

35. **Execution**. This could be termed executive talent, as it concerns the ability to create and run some kind of enterprise. There is a kind of destructive or revolutionary aspect to this bump which suggests that if it is overlarge, the subject would seek to break down the existing status quo and impose one of his own making. A small bump here signifies an inefficient and ineffective type of person who wants peace at any price.

36. **Combativeness**. Resistance, courage, and the ability to stand up for oneself. If the bump is overlarge, the subject will be aggressive, if very small he will be a coward.

37. **Vitativeness**. The will to live life to the full. With a very large bump, the subject would struggle for survival against any odds. If it is very small, he may have little tenacity and no great desire to live. A lack of a bump here could indicate suicidal tendencies.

Area F

38. **Friendship**. The ability to be sociable and to make friends. If the bump is overlarge, the subject will be indiscriminate and overfriendly. If small, he will be unfriendly.

39. **Conjugality**. The ability to make lasting relationships or to make a success of marriage. A normal or large bump here belongs to a relater, while a small one denotes a loner. If the Amativeness (No. 40) bump is large and the Conjugality bump small, the subject will want love and sex without having to work at a steady relationship.

40. **Amativeness**. This rules the sexual instincts. If large, the subject will be a sensualist—an overlarge bump here denotes that someone prizes sexual conquests over other forms of relationships. If small, the subject will lack sensuality or sexual desire.

Area G

41. **Inhabitiveness**. A love of home life and also a love of one's country. If overdeveloped, this subject could hang on to his home at any cost, or he (or she) could make a great fuss of the home and its contents. If the bump is small, the subject may be something of a drifter with little regard for a home or even for his country.

42. **Philoprogenitiveness**. A love of and desire for children—also a love of pets. If the bump is very large, this person might relate better to children and pets than to adults. If small, he will not be interested in either children or pets.

10

Face Reading

Face reading is a well known ancient Chinese art, but there is some evidence that a form of face reading was also known in Europe in the 19th century. This chapter gives a little information on both the Chinese and European systems. Unlike the previous chapter on phrenology, face reading can indicate the kind of fortune a person can expect as well as giving some indication as to his character.

To some extent, we all read faces all the time. When we look at someone who is new to us, we unconsciously assess him or her and form our initial opinions. In addition to our instinctive need to read faces, there exist far more detailed methods of incorporating rules that have been carefully worked out over a long period of time. The best exponents of this skill are undoubtedly the Chinese; since this a deep and difficult subject to master, but in this book I shall just dip into the subject in order to give you a brief introduction to a fascinating skill; see Further Reading for other resources.

Chinese face reading

The Chinese call the forehead area down to the eyebrows *heaven*, and this is associated with the early years of life. The middle area is called *human*, and this is associated with the middle years. The lower section, from the base of the nose down to the bottom of the face is termed *earth*, and this is concerned with old age.

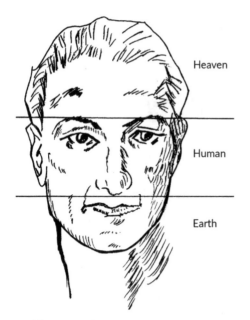

Heaven

Human

Earth

Any part of the face that is scarred, malformed, or discolored suggests a problem in the area of the subject's life that is associated with that segment of the face. Gray or black marks, whether permanent or temporary, denote problems that are themselves either permanent or temporary. Even if a discoloration is caused by a trick of the light, it will mean something. In every form of divination, intuition plays its part, so if yours kicks in while trying out this form of divination, allow it to flow through.

Heaven

Positive: If this area is clean, clear, and well developed, the subject will have a good start in life with wonderful parents and a useful education.

Negative: Scarring, dents, or discoloration here indicate a troubled childhood and a poor education. The problems will be worse for a man if the disfigurement is on the left and for a woman if it is on the right. A wide forehead is generally considered to be beneficial—but in a woman, a very wide forehead suggests poor personal relationships. The lines on the forehead can be lucky or unfortunate, depending upon where they are situated.

Human

Positive: The middle section of the subject's life will be happy and productive, with stability in relationships and success in the career.

Negative: The opposite of the positive reading. A human section that is longer than either of the other two represents a determined and self-disciplined personality.

Earth

Positive: A happy old age with good relationships with children and grandchildren. Prosperity in life and a comfortable old age.

Negative: The opposite of the positive reading.

The thirteen divisions of the face

The Chinese further divide the face into thirteen subsections. Here is a very simplified version of the thirteen-section reading, starting from the top of the face and working downward.

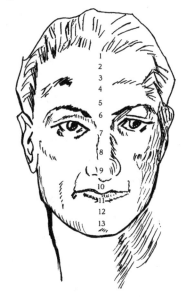

1. If this is clean and clear, the subject will have a happy childhood and youth and a good relationship with his parents, who should live to a ripe old age. If it is marked or misshapen, there will be unhappiness in youth due to poverty or discord within the childhood home. Veins, dark marks, and so forth here signify accidents and sudden losses of money and prestige. A widow's peak suggests that the father will die before the mother.
2. This is similar to the above, but it talks more about the mother than the father. Negatively, a marked area suggests that the subject will not be believed when he is telling the truth.

3. A good complexion here indicates a fortunate and successful life, whereas discoloration tells of a bad patch in the subject's career.

4. If this is dented, the intellect will be low. If scarred, bumpy, or sporting a mole, the subject will be impatient and largely unable to bring his plans to fruition as a result of bad public relations skills or bad luck. He will also find it hard to make and keep friends.

5. If this area is healthy, the subject will receive an inheritance and he will succeed in business. Eyebrows that meet or almost meet denote failure, bad luck, and a lack of respect from other people. Marks, scars, and black moles can indicate anything from adoption to sickness and failure—even a term of imprisonment! Wrinkles or creases between the eyebrows are considered to be all right if the subject is over forty years of age, otherwise they denote difficulties, tension, and possibly a jealous nature.

6. Grayness here denotes sickness; whereas a green patch at the side indicates adultery. A mole suggests stomach problems, emigration, or even imprisonment!

7. Moles here suggest stomach trouble, relationship problems, or possibly a partner who is sick. Darkness here tells of a sickly child.

8. A high bony nose suggests failure in business. Moles and discoloration signify a sick husband and difficulties with females.

9. The tip of the nose should be full in shape and clear of marks, hairs, and blackheads for good fortune.

10. This is the groove between the base of the nose and the mouth. If the base of the groove is wider than the upper part and the indentation is neither too deep or too flat, the subject will have healthy children and he will achieve a high level of wealth and status in life. If it is wider at the top and shallow in shape, the subject will experience difficulties in having children, and his nature may be sour and ill-mannered. Relationships will be difficult. If the area is

bent, the subject will be childless and he will also be deceitful and unpopular. A straight line that is marked down the middle of the groove denotes children late in life.

11. The mouth. This should be reasonably full with a pinkish color and upturned corners to ensure prosperity, good health, and a happy marriage.

12. If this area is dark in the morning, the subject should avoid traveling across water during the course of that day. A man who has a hairless gap beneath his lower lip or a person of either sex who has a scar or discoloration in this area must be careful of their diet, as their stomach may be weak.

13. This should be round, slightly protuberant, and strong in appearance. A sharp chin is unlucky. If the chin points to the side, the subject will hold grudges against others. Any scarring or discoloration denotes money losses, possibly the loss of an inheritance. This can also foretell family sickness and accidents.

English face reading

Face shapes

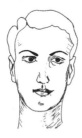  

Round or oval: A pleasant, friendly person who needs a good home and family life. Good judgement and intuitive faculties and a desire for justice and fair play. This person can work hard and is capable and efficient, but he can also relax when necessary. A well-balanced personality.

Square or rectangular face: Dynamic, determined, and capable. This person has leadership qualities and physical strength. Strong-willed, opinionated, intelligent, and tough. Dexterous, mechanically minded, and active. This subject would make a good soldier.

Triangular or heart shaped: Sensitive, creative, intellectual, and with a good mind and memory. Can be hard to understand due to moodiness. A dreamer who needs direction in life. Restless and easily bored.

Round/triangular: Intellectual and businesslike but also restless and moody. Overoptimistic and overconfident at times. Finds honest self-assessment difficult.

Round/square: Active, cheerful, opinionated, and egotistical but also capable and businesslike.

Square/triangular: Clever, impetuous, inventive, active. Prospers as a result of creativity.

Side view profiles

Concave: Steady, rather inflexible. Appears deep and clever but may not

be so. Wastes time fiddling about with minor matters. Reserved, interested in the past, good memory.

Convex: Lively, clever, quick thinking. A talker and doer rather than a listener. Practical, quick-on-the-uptake, active. Soon becomes bored and restless, so needs variety in his daily life and in his job.

Straight: Calm, deliberate, reasonable, and patient but stubborn, tenacious, and strongly opinionated. Has the patience to work things out thoroughly. (I have noticed over the years that many actors on film and television have a straight profile, which confirms that they have the patience to learn lines and put up with the utter boredom of filming.)

The forehead

If this is well proportioned and free of marks, scars, and discoloration, the subject will have a good start in life and a good relationship with his parents. Otherwise a large forehead denotes a deep thinker, while a narrow forehead denotes an analytical thinker. A forehead that is flat or dented inward suggests good concentration and a cautious temperament, while one that bulges outward suggests shrewdness and good powers of observation. A low forehead is supposed to indicate a nature that is practical rather than intellectual.

The eyebrows

Clean, clear, and gently curving brows indicate refinement, humor, intelligence, and a lucky life. Curved eyebrows suggest an inquiring mind and arched ones or those that flip up and then down at the ends, indicate a creative imagination. Busy ones belong to more temperamental types, who can be unpleasant at times, while very thin ones denote a fussy nature. Upwardly sloping brows signify ambition, while tufted ones indicate pleasure in hurting others. Downwardly sloping brows represent a lack of energy and a tendency to whine. Widely spaced brows show refinement and adaptability, whereas close ones denote a hot temper, energy, and determination.

The eyes

The eyes are considered to be such an important feature that "good" eyes can mitigate the effects of poor features. Eyes that dart about restlessly belong to a dishonest person, and someone who cannot meet your eyes is cunning. (I have also noticed that these darting eyes denote a lack of self-confidence and sometimes also craziness.)

Crows feet around the eyes in an older person suggest the ability to solve problems, while in a young person they denote laziness. A person who has no fold in the eyelid will overreact to emotional situations, while someone who has the white showing all around the eye either has a severe thyroid problem—or a cunning, untrustworthy, and bad-tempered personality. Oval eyes suggest a good temper and a sharp mind, while round ones indicate a nature that is naïve and trusting. Slanted eyes denote secretiveness and a sly nature, as do narrowed eyes. Eyes that are wide apart signify openness and tolerance, whilst eyes that are close together suggest intolerance and a fairly tough attitude to the self and to others. Protuberant eyes denote creativity but also laziness, and deep-set eyes indicate tenacity but a lack of creativity. Small eyes indicate materialism, greed, a money-minded nature, a love of luxury, and a person who will do anything or put up with anything for an easy and comfortable life. Alternatively, small eyes can indicate good concentration and the ability to finish whatever the person starts.

11

Graphology

Graphology, the art of reading handwriting, is unique among divinations because the establishment actually accepts it. The police and legal profession use handwriting experts to check on forgeries, while firms the world over use them to check out prospective employees. There are even graphologists who specialize in analyzing ancient documents, both in order to date them and translate them; these experts can also tell which ancient scripts were written by the same person or otherwise.

The appearance of the page

Messy writing denotes a messy mind, but this may be a temporary situation brought on by stress. First drafts of anything are usually messy because the writer is not considering the appearance of his work but simply getting his thoughts down quickly. A person whose writing has remained unchanged since he was at school has not developed his personality or achieved any measure of individuality. The more handwriting changes after it has first been learned, the more developed the individual's personality.

Margins

If the margins are even, the subject has a tidy mind and an artistic eye. If the left margin is narrow, he is reserved and hypersensitive, while if the right margin is narrow he is generous and reckless. A page that is absolutely covered by writing either suggests stinginess or a person who has a lot to say. A page with extremely wide margins indicates a fearful, repressed, and fastidious personality.

Direction

If the writing line wanders upward, the subject is optimistic and healthy at the time of writing. If it slopes downward, pessimism or illness are indicated. Words that rise upward indicate happiness; a downward slope indicates unhappiness.

Spacing

If the spacing between words is wide, the subject wants to keep others at a distance. If it is very close he may be possessive, clinging, or hostile.

Size

It is normal for a young person to have large writing, but in an older person it means that he is either immature or that he wishes to impress people and to impose his personality on them. Small writing indicates that the writer has a reserved, introverted nature and the academic, detailed mind of a researcher. If the writing increases in size as it goes along, the subject has an open nature and he will be tactless. If it decreases in size, he is secretive and he may be a liar.

Shape

Wide writing belongs to an active, outgoing person who loves to travel but who has little consideration for others. Lean writing belongs to a pedantic person who appreciates work that is well thought out. Square writing belongs to a mathematical type and round writing indicates sociability and a loving nature. Connected writing indicates a logical mind while disconnected writing denotes an artistic and intuitive mind.

The slant of the letters

People with upright writing are organized, sensible, and responsible as well as sociable and pleasant. They will help themselves and also others when asked. A slight slant to the right shows that the subject needs people in his life. He is also outgoing and an extrovert if the writing is large, although more introverted if it is medium or small. A right slant also indicates a good head for business. A great deal of right slant shows that the subject is easily bored, restless, and that he has many acquaintances. A slight left slant suggests that the subject is thoughtful, introspective, and slightly introverted. A good deal of left slant shows too much vulnerability and introspection. This person is a dreamer and he is very loyal to those whom he loves.

Zones

Graphologists divide letters into three zones.

Upper zone
Middle zone
Lower zone

The upper zone is formed by loops or lines that reach upward in such letters as d, h, l, k, and t. The middle zone is formed by the main area of script. The lower zone is formed by the tails of letters such as g, p, y, and z.

The upper zone gives us an insight into the subject's dreams, ambitions, ideals, aims, and spiritual aspirations. The middle zone concerns daily life, relationships, work, and general social behavior. The lower zone relates to sex and other basic requirements such as food and security. This can also relate to physical movement (as in sports, etc.) and such things as possessiveness, acquisitiveness, and materialism.

The upper zone

Average: The subject's aims, ambitions, dreams, and outlooks are normal.

Tall: The subject is interested in intellectual pursuits, he is idealistic and he may be impractical and out of touch with reality. He will also be vain, proud, and sensitive to criticism.

Short: The subject is practical, interested in mundane daily life, and rarely looks beyond the obvious. Mentally alert but unable to apply his ideas.

Loops: Loops on letters such as h, d, l, etc. denote creative thought. Straight lines suggest either a more practical and logical type of person or a person who may be temporarily stifling his creativity.

The middle zone

Large: The subject seeks to impress others and he is keen to have their approval. He is sociable, practical, and he avoids acting on instinct. (He or she may also simply be young.)

Small: This subject is an instinctive, academic type who works to his own standards and does not seek approval or seek to impress others.

The lower zone

Large: The subject is a physical person who is interested in sports, gardening, or sex. He has plenty of energy and he may be rash and self-opinionated.

Loops: If the loops are wide, the subject will be aggressive, combative, and materialistic. If they are angular, he could be angry, obstreperous, and difficult or he could have sexual problems. Straight lines instead of loops indicate a person who is moody and unhappy, who hates physical activity, and is lazy and apt to speak in short sentences or not have much to say. Alternatively, this person might be artistic, musical, or mechanical.

The I's have it

I   *A clear-thinking person who is interested in mechanics and engineering.*

ı   *The concise type who deals only with essentials.*

ℓ   *This subject is either self-important or very intellectual.*

y   *A physical, outdoor type of person.*

∩   *This one avoids responsibility.*

ʒ   *A bit full of himself, but otherwise reasonable.*

ʒ   *Pleasant and humorous with an open, friendly nature.*

Capital letters

Large capitals show a big ego and small ones suggest a small one. Ornamental capitals belong to someone who is vain or who is an unusual personality. Capitals that lean all over the rest of the writing show an aggressive and fussy personality.

A A   *This A shows kindness and sympathy.*

A A   *This A shows balance and common sense.*

B   *This closed B will not be taken in or swindled by others.*

B   *This open B is gullible.*

D Σ   *These lead-in strokes show an aggressive, irritable, impatient nature, a person who is proud and status conscious.*

P R   *Broken capitals show open-mindedness and generosity.*

P R   *Closed capitals show a cautious, cheap-skate nature.*

M   *"Painted" letters show an artistic nature.*

Lower-case letters

a *a*   Bigheartedness, generosity, and a nature that is too open.

a *o*   Secretiveness and the ability to keep confidences.

a *c* *s*   The lead-in stroke shows petulance and irritability—also a person who is slow to warm up sexually.

b *b*   The open b shows generosity and gullibility; the closed one is cautious and tightfisted.

g   Literary ability and a quick mind.

d *d*   A loop on the d shows sensitive feelings; the lack of a loop indicates a person who does not worry about other people's opinion of him.

t *t*   The same as for the d above.

f *t*   A loop missing on the f shows a sound mind. Two loops missing suggest that the subject is artistic and clever with his hands.

h *k*   An angular h can indicate aggression or a sharp intellect, while an angular k is always a sign of an aggressive personality.

m *n* *w*   Rounded letters denote gentleness and also someone who is good with his hands.

m *n* *w*   Angular writing indicates a person who has an active mind, a love of efficiency, and who is enthusiastic about what he does.

p *p*   An open p belongs to a straightforward, gentle person who enjoys the simple things of life. A loop on the down-stroke shows that the subject desires to be more mobile or out of doors.

r *r*   This represents a proud, awkward person.

r   A gentle, thoughtful person.

r   When the r looks like a printed letter, the subject is clever and versatile.

S	A quick mind with many interests and no lack of ability. Also a tenacious person who will not be pushed around.
$\mathcal{A}$	The closed s denotes great caution.
$\sim$	A yielding nature.
$\ell \;\; \hbar$	Wide loops—this person is overemotional, histrionic, and hysterical. Possibly also a good actor.
$\mathcal{l}$	Narrow loops indicate suppressed emotion.
$b \;\; \mathcal{l} \;\; \hbar$	Lines instead of loops denote good judgment and a head that rules the heart. A rapid thinker who probably has a good education.
$g \;\; y$	Tiny lower loops signify a lack of vitality.
$g \;\; y$	Large lower loops show a vital person who enjoys exercise, sports, or dancing.
$\mathcal{f} \;\; \mathcal{f}$	Angular loops demonstrate determination and forcefulness.
$\mathcal{f}$	Large angular loops signify a tendency to exaggerate, be pompous and boastful, and to enjoy ordering people around.
$\mathcal{q} \;\; \mathcal{y}$	No loops at all show a mind that rules the heart and a mental rather than a physical personality.
$\mathcal{f} \;\; \mathcal{f}$	A multiplication of loops shows temporary or permanent insanity. This person may be a liar or a deceiver and will not be popular.
$\mathcal{y} \;\; \mathcal{g}$	Flicks instead of loops denote a person who is persnickety about appearances, a fuss-pot, and petty-minded about small matters.

Signatures

Very often the signature is different from other handwriting. There may also be different names or different ways of signing things according to what it is. For example I use a small, right-slant "S Fenton" scrawl for checks, credit cards, official documents, and so forth, where formality is important. This is the signature that I used before becoming a well-known writer. I habitually use a middle-sized, upright, and clearly written "Sasha Fenton" for business letters, signing books, or anything to do with my work. In the first case, this is for convenience, while in the second case, I guess I am saying, "This is who I am and this is what I do." If my personality were less important to my work, I probably wouldn't have instinctively chosen to use such a signature.

If the signature is clearly legible, the subject is honest and open. If it is illegible, he may be hiding something or he may just be shy. If the forename is larger and more strongly emphasized, he will want to put things on a personal basis but if the surname is emphasized, he will want to keep things formal. A dot after the signature shows a tidy mind but also the need for approval or to impress others. A line below shows self-importance, but it will be put there unconsciously in some cases to compensate for the lack of lower-loop letters in the signature. Twirly bits are put there to draw attention to the subject and to show how special he is.

A signature with a soft appearance denotes a gentle personality, while a more angular or aggressive one shows a tougher and more difficult personality. A line that leads into the signature shows that the subject is clinging to the past while a line that tails out at the end shows tact, kindness, or generosity. If the signature is placed in the middle of the page or to the left, the subject is shy or introverted; if it is on the right, he is cheerful and outgoing.

12

Moles

Years ago people considered that the position of a mole on the body signified certain characteristics for a person and also a particular kind of outlook for the future. I have reproduced the ideas in this chapter from an early 19th century script that clearly has roots that go back much further than that. After checking out people and their moles, I have to say that most of this stuff is pretty silly—but annoyingly, some of it is spot-on. Please don't take the more frightening interpretations literally, but simply have a bit of fun with this rather daft form of divination.

The size, color, and shape of the mole must be taken into consideration because while a collection of pale freckles won't mean anything, an isolated and obvious mole will. The larger the mole, the more important it is. If a mole is round, its effects will be beneficial; an oblong mole is fairly lucky, but an angular one is considered to be a bad omen. A dark mole has a stronger effect than a pale one. A very hairy one is considered to be a very bad omen indeed, while a couple of hairs on a mole bring prosperity.

I hardly need to add that if a mole becomes itchy, crusty, or starts to spread you must visit your doctor immediately, as this could be an indication of skin cancer.

Location of Moles

- A mole on the right side of the forehead shows that the person is going places in his career.

- On the right eyebrow, the subject will marry when young and his or her partner will be very pleasant to live with.

- On the left side of either the forehead or the eyebrow, unexpected disappointment.

- A mole on the outside corner of either eye denotes that the subject is steady, sober, and reliable.

- A mole on either cheek means that the subject will never be rich but he won't be particularly poor either.

- A mole on the nose suggests success in all undertakings.

- One on the lip means that the subject is stylish and fastidious and also lucky in matters of love.

- On the chin, this shows luck and success in career and business matters. This person will reach a position of great status.

- A mole on the neck means that the subject will narrowly avoid being suffocated!

- On the throat, wealth through marriage.

- On the right side of the chest or back, a fall in status and income. This also means that most of the subject's children will be girls.

- On the left side of the chest or back, success in business and a high level of sexuality.

- A woman with a mole on the breast will have a mediocre life with no great gains or losses.

- A man with a mole on the left side of the chest over the heart denotes a kindly person who likes to ramble on. He is often slightly discontented, as he tends to chew things over too much in his mind.

- In a woman, a mole under the left breast suggests that she will carry and give birth to children without difficulty.

- A mole, which is low down on the right side of the ribs, suggests a slow thinker who is best left to do things at his own pace.

- A mole on the belly belongs to a selfish, greedy, gluttonous, and lazy person. This subject is also slovenly and dirty.

- A mole that is fairly low down on the back means a lifetime of hard work. (I have discovered that this one is absolutely true, as everyone I have encountered who works hard seems to have such a mole.)

- A mole on the hip means that the person will have many children who will be patient, hardworking, and who will turn out to be a credit to him.

- On the right thigh, riches plus a happy and lucky marriage.

- On the left thigh, poverty and a lack of friends. This subject is also on the receiving end of hatred and injustice from others.

- On the right knee, an easy life and a good marriage.

- On the left knee, a temper that can result in rash acts, but under normal circumstances a cool, honest, and decent person.

- On either calf, a lazy thoughtless person who lives for today and who doesn't think forward.

- A mole on either ankle suggests that a male subject will be somewhat feminine or even effeminate in his manner, while a female will be courageous, active, and a real termagant!

13

Itches

We are all know that when one of our ears is itching or burning it means that someone is talking about us or that when our right palm itches that money is on the way. However, we are not as familiar with other "itchy" wives tales and other similar bodily omens.

Most itches are momentary things that go away as quickly as they come and they have no special significance, but some need to be taken seriously. In fact, any persistent itch deserves a visit to the doctor. For example, regular episodes of itching or burning in the feet (especially during the night) can be a symptom of diabetes. Ongoing itchiness on the arms and legs can also signal diabetes. A persistent itch on the back (toward the lower end of the left shoulder blade) can denote heart disease. A pregnant woman with a severe and constant itch on her hands must seek immediate medical advice. If her doctor doesn't take her worries seriously, she must insist on consulting a specialist because this kind of itch can indicate a condition that causes stillbirth. However, please use common sense here, as the occasional itch or other bodily event usually means nothing—apart from the amusing meanings given in the following list.

- If the crown of your head itches, promotion and an increase in salary are on the way.

- If you comb your hair and find it coming away in large amounts, you will soon be seriously ill. (This has a basis in fact: when illness looms, the body sheds hair in a kind of energy saving campaign.)

- If your right eyebrow itches, you will soon meet up again with an old friend or be reunited with a previous lover.

- If your left eyebrow itches, you will soon meet a friend who is sick or you will see your old lover with someone else.

- A ringing in your right ear means that you will soon hear good news.

- A ringing in your left ear means that you will soon hear bad news. When your left ear tingles, someone is maligning your name.

- A violent itching of the nose means that trouble and worry are on the way. (Or hay fever perhaps?)

- Itchy lips mean that someone is running you down behind your back.

- An itch on the back of your neck means that someone close to you is about to suffer a violent death. (Don't take this one seriously!)

- An itchy right shoulder means that you will shortly receive a large legacy.

- An itchy left shoulder means that you will soon be weighed down with troubles.

- If your right elbow itches, good news is on the way.

- If your left elbow itches, you will suffer a disappointment.

- If your right palm is itchy, there is money on the way to you.

- If your left palm itches, you will have to pay someone else's debts.

- An itchy spine denotes heavy burdens being on the way to you.

- An itching of the genital region means that you will shortly have an addition to your family, or that you will shortly be married.

- If your tummy itches, you can expect to eat a sumptuous meal.

- If one or both your thighs itch, you will soon be sleeping elsewhere.

- If your right knee itches, your life will change for the better and you will become interested in some kind of religion.

- If your left knee itches, you will have a setback in life.

- If your shins itch, you will have a long and painful illness. (Another one that is not worth taking seriously!)

- If your ankle joints itch, you will be united or reunited with a loved one. If you are already happily settled, your life will become even happier.

- If the sole of your right foot itches, you will soon be on a pleasant journey.

- If the sole of your left foot itches, you will soon be on a sad or unpleasant journey.

- Finally, if you find yourself unaccountably depressed, you will soon be hearing some good news.

14

Pendulums

Pendulums (and dowsing rods) are usually used to locate things, but
they can also be used in order to discover a straight *yes* or *no* answer
to a question. Rods can be used to find underground sources of
water, drain pipes, sources of specific minerals, and lost objects. A pendulum can be used to identify an illness or spot a dietary deficiency. Pendu-
lums can be held over a map or a sketch of a specific place in order to find
someone or something.

Preparation and Ritual

Before using a new pendulum, hold it in your hands and ask your spiritual
guides to help you to use it in a caring and truthful manner. Imagine yourself calling down a shaft of white light from the universe, mentally allow
this to settle around your feet, and then wind it up around your body in a
clockwise direction.

Once you have prepared your pendulum, you will have to establish
which kind of movement will be your *yes* and which will be your *no*. Take
your pendulum and wind the string or chain around your little finger and
hold your hand with the palm uppermost. Then allow the chain to run
across the underside of your fingers and then down over your index finger.
Now think *yes*. The pendulum may move backwards, side to side, or in a
circle. The movement will be in direct response to your brain patterns and
nerve endings, because the pendulum and you are merely channels for

your guides to use. The pendulum does not have any life itself, other than the receptive energy that you charged it with when you went through the preparation ritual. After doing this, go through the same exercise again, this time thinking *no*, and this will give you your *no* movement. You can now form a question in your mind, but remember to couch this in such a manner as to receive a straight *yes* or *no* answer. (If using dowsing rods, hold them out in front of you at a comfortable distance from your body and think *yes*. If the rods cross, this will be your *yes* or if they part then that will be your *yes*.)

If you are trying to diagnose an ailment, you can dowse over the body of the person, or you can dowse over a drawing of a body representing the person. Start by holding the pendulum over the head and slowly draw it down the body, and the area of the body that is sick will set off a movement in the pendulum. Dowsing for allergies is a more specific divination because you will need to buy a book that shows exactly what length of thread your pendulum needs to be held at in order to discover what it is that the person is allergic to.

Another way to dowse for a specific sickness is to write a list of the most likely ailments, leaving plenty of space between the words. Then take your pendulum and dowse over the list, and if the person has one of the ailments on the list, the pendulum will register your *yes* position.

Ley Lines

You may have read that there are specific energy lines called ley lines that cross a country, but there are many minor ley lines as well. If you suspect that your sleeping position or your desk placement doesn't suit you, you can dowse for a negative line in that area. Simply take your pendulum and think "ley line." If it finds one it will indicate "yes." Now do it again thinking "negative ley line," and if get a "yes" response, you know you have discovered a negative ley line. Simply moving your bed, desk, chair, or other piece of furniture to a different part of the room or to a different room could improve your life.

Choices

Just as you can dowse over a list of ailments, so can you dowse over a list of any other kind. If you have several choices to make or if you want to know the answer to anything, just write a variety of answers down on a piece of paper, leaving plenty of space between the lines and then dowse over them. The right choice or the answer to your question will set the pendulum into action.

15

Dream Interpretation

Scientists tell us that we dream every time we sleep. Sleep deepens and lightens in fairly fixed periods with around ninety minutes of deep sleep, interspersed with blocks of fifteen or twenty minutes of lighter sleep. Dreaming is the mind's way of sifting through and processing the impressions with which it has been bombarded throughout the day, keeping those that are relevant and rejecting those that are not.

It is worth looking for a logical reason for a bad dream before jumping to the conclusion that it means something ominous. It used to be said that eating cheese before going to bed caused bad dreams! Certainly too much alcohol or food can give one a bad night, while pain or a high temperature are bound to disturb one's sleep. Every now and then, a dream will keep popping up to haunt you over a period of several weeks, and in this case there is definitely something significant to consider.

Many dreams tell us something about our state of mind, perhaps bringing to our attention things that are at the back of our minds that we don't wish to consciously acknowledge. I remember someone telling me that she was happy to be planning her wedding and looking forward to being married to her fiancé, but every night she dreamed that she was locked away in prison. This lady's subconscious was clearly telling her that she was getting herself into a difficult situation that would be hard to escape from—and so it turned out.

Stress dreams can include going somewhere only to find that we have forgotten something vital, or are not prepared for an exam, or we're trying to get into a car and are not able to, or perhaps trying to stop a car that is rolling down the street. There are many variations of these and they all relate to stress in some way. Many dreams are known as *contrary* dreams, which means that a bad dream may actually be an indication of good fortune being on the way.

Occult significance

Of course, there are dreams that have a specific occult significance. These might warn of a forthcoming problem or predict a particular event. Before the Arab terrorists crashed their airplanes into the World Trade Center, many psychic and sensitive people, had dreams about it—and I was one of them. There may be a symbolic dream that hides a specific meaning. A common example is dreaming of a broken wedding ring, which signifies uncertainty about a marriage or relationship.

Health

The Chinese believe that certain kinds of dreams indicate particular health problems. For instance they believe that dreams of terror indicate heart problems, while dreams of bloodshed relate to the lungs. Dreaming of hacking one's way through the jungle signifies liver problems and dreaming of sharp pain indicates kidney disorders. Dreams of some kind of repetitious action, such as swinging backwards and forwards signify anemia. A single dream of this kind is probably fairly meaningless, but if such dreams recur or persist, then it might be worth taking them seriously and having a check-up.

• • •

The following list shows some traditional dream interpretations. This is purely divinatory and it doesn't take any kind of deep psychological meaning into account. Although this kind of divination is meant only as a bit of fun, I have found it to work quite well. There are plenty of books around that cover every conceivable kind of dream. Full sized books will also give longer interpretations to the dreams than I can give in this one.

Dream Interpretation List

Dreams about babies

Baby: Good luck for the dreamer and his family.

Birth: Good fortune.

Cradle: Hopes and wishes to be fulfilled.

Pregnancy: Good news is on the way.

Dreams about marriage

Bells: Good news.

Bouquet: Slight disappointment.

Horseshoe: A pleasant journey.

Wedding: Joy and happiness ahead.

Dreams of death

These are amazingly common, and different sources give different interpretations but most seem to consider these lucky, although some are not. Death in many occult beliefs indicates a fresh start or the transformation of something that is ready to die off into something new and better.

Burial: The dreamer will soon be married.

Cemetery: The dreamer will hear of a death.

Death: Turning point, transformation, good fortune, and happiness.

Gallows: Prosperity.

Shipwreck: Hesitation and disappointments.

Tomb: A long, happy life foretold.

Dreams about men

Doctor: Illness is on the way.

Friend: Good luck and happiness.

Horseman: Plans fulfilled.

Lawyer: A warning of legal or financial difficulties.

Old man: Happiness for the family.

Policeman: Peace and safety.

Postman: Long awaited news.

Sailor: Difficulties or delays in plans.

Dreams about women

Actress: Deception from those whom you trust.

Empress: Both status and success or pride causes a fall.

Nun: Peace of mind.

Witch: Difficulties in the near future.

Dreams of friends

Drowning friend: Someone will render the dreamer a service.

Friend's house: Good luck in work and other plans.

Friend in difficulty: Either your friend will need help, or you will need your friend to help you.

Dreams about children

Children playing: Happiness is on the way.

Crying child: A wish will be fulfilled.

Dancing child: Difficulties ahead.

Death of a child: A welcome visitor.

Sleeping child: Good luck is coming to the dreamer.

Dreams about animals, birds, insects, and fish

Ants: Hard work ahead, but the results will be worthwhile.

Bat: Danger threatens.

Bear: Disagreements with friends.

Bees: Prosperity and progress.

Cat: Beware of treachery.

Cockerel: Success and joy are on the way.

Cow: Prosperity.

Crab: A parting.

Dog: Malicious gossip.

Donkey: Trouble in store.

Dove: Peace and happiness in love.

Duck: A stranger brings bad news.

Eagle: Success.

Elephant: Plans will succeed.

Fish: Unexpected news.

Fox: Plans will succeed beyond your wildest expectations.

Goose: Someone whom you love will let you down.

Hedgehog: Business difficulties and complications.

Hen: Celebrations and parties.

Horse: Black horse: Disappointments. Brown house: Stagnation and delays. White horse: Financial progress.

Lamb: Wishes will come true.

Lion: You will soon take the lead in an important enterprise.

Parrot: A trusted friend will quarrel with you.

Peacock: Wealth coming through the family.

Rabbit: You will soon make a good and useful friend.

Rat: A supposed friend is working against you. Women should beware of becoming entangled with a "rat."

Snake: Gossip. However, this is good news for love affairs.

Spider: Danger of being involved in a quarrel.

Swallow: Domestic circumstances will change a little.

Swan: Financial progress and happiness.

Tiger: Hidden danger threatens. (Oddly enough, tigers tend to feature when we have a high temperature, so this could indicate the onset of influenza or something similar.)

Toad: Hidden danger.

Vulture: Sickness in the family.

Wolf: Business losses and worries.

Worms: A number of small worries.

Dreams about conditions

Applause: A friend will rebuke the dreamer.

Attack: Rashness will cause difficulties.

Battle: Health worries.

Climbing: Success coming, albeit slowly.

Competition: It will soon be easier to attain ambitions.

Dancing: Pleasure, parties, and dancing.

Dispute: Take care, be cautious.

Exile: Loss of something or someone valuable.

Falling: A confusing time is ahead.

Finding money: Loss.

Flying: Advancement in circumstances and/or a desire to escape.

Following one's own funeral: Turning point, transformation, great and lasting success.

Gambling: Success coming soon.

Honors: Beware of slander.

Imprisonment: Delays and problems that are hard to resolve. This could also be a warning against getting into a difficult situation in the near future.

Kidnapping: Success in plans.

Legacy: Financial loss.

Murder: Successful outcome in plans.

Nakedness: Financial loss.

Poverty: Change for the better.

Presents: Loss that wipes out previous gains.

Reading: Pleasure coming from a new source.

Screaming: Bad news coming.

Shopping: Unexpected benefit coming.

Singing: Success in endeavors.

Suicide: Upheaval and major changes.

Swimming: Improvement after a bad patch.

Travel: Friends will let the dreamer down.

Undressing: Lack of foresight will cause problems.

Visiting: A grave injustice is on the way.

Wealth: Disillusionment.

Weeping: Good news is on the way.

Wrestling: The dreamer will win through.

Writing: Danger of offending a friend.

Dreams about money

Finding money: Difficulties are on the way.

Losing money: Plans will succeed beyond the dreamer's wildest hopes.

Counting money: Gains coming.

Spending money: Losses on the way.

Dreams about health

Amputation: Slights and injustices.

Asthma: Difficulties ahead.

Burns: Success coming and an end of troubles.

Loss of a tooth: Loss of a friend or relative.

Problems with feet: Prosperity.

Problems with hands: Parting from a good friend.

Ulcer: Temporary difficulty.

General dream list

Airplane: Ambition to be fulfilled.

Ambulance: Sickness in the family.

Axe: Help from a friend.

Bag: Full: Prosperity. Empty: Hard times ahead.

Ball: Great moves forward.

Bank: Money worries.

Barrel: Full: Improvement in circumstances. Empty: Money worries.

Basket: A welcome invitation.

Bath: Happiness to come.

Beans: Danger to the family.

Bed: If made: Rest. If unmade: Take care, avoid trouble.

Bell: Good news, joy.

Blood: An accident.

Boat: News, a successful journey.

Bridge: Troubles will soon pass.

Buttons: Peace and joy in the family.

Candle: Lighted: A birth in the family. Extinguished: A death in the dreamer's circle.

Castle: Unexpectedly pleasurable event.

Chain: Difficulties.

Church: Peace after a period of trouble.

Clock: Business matters that require the dreamer's attention.

Clouds: Quarrels with friends.

Coal: The dreamer will impress his superiors.

Cottage: Health and happiness.

Crown: Honors.

Crossroads: Important decisions to be made.

Dice: Beware of taking a gamble, as losses are possible.

Dungeon: Danger for those around the dreamer.

Earthquake: Someone close to you is running a risk.

Eggs: An up-turn in finances, also good health.

Eyes: A lover is on the way or the dreamer's current love life will improve.

Factory: The dreamer's efforts will be rewarded.

Fingers: Litigation concerning money.

Fire: Unexpected happy event.

Fireplace: Someone will go away.

Flag: A change in life brings success.

Flowers: A trip or a move to the countryside.

Fountain: A busy time is ahead.

Glass: Full: The dreamer will soon hear from a loved one. Empty: Temporary difficulties. Broken: Wishes will come true. If appropriate, a wedding.

Globe: A worthwhile journey.

Gun: Danger, disappointment, or limited success.

Hammer: Recklessness will cause problems.

Hand: The dreamer will be surrounded by flatterers.

Hat: Disappointment.

House: This shows the state of the dreamer's mind. The house in the dream will probably be different from the one he lives in. The condition of the house in the dream should be taken into consideration. For instance, is it large, small, tidy, messy, lonely, or filled with party goers—and what kinds of emotions are prevalent in the dream?

Island: Loneliness to come.

Jewels: A raise in status and an upturn in finances.

Key: The dreamer must prepare for any upcoming interview so that he makes the best of himself.

Kitchen: Improvement in finances. Like the **house** dream, the state of the kitchen reflects the state of the dreamer's mind.

Knife: Danger for the dreamer or for a loved one.

Knot: Complications in affairs.

Ladder: Patience will bring success.

Lamp: Lit: Good for business affairs. Extinguished: Concealment of something important from the dreamer.

Lighthouse: Good advice is on the way.

Linen (dirty): Arguments in the family—don't wash dirty linen in public.

Lock: Guard against theft.

Map: Long journey.

Meat: Raw: Prosperity. Cooked: Disappointment.

Mirror: Flattery from the opposite sex.

Milk: In a glass or jug: Tranquility. Spilt: Plans will not work out.

Moon: Something will work out within a month.

Mountain: Work brings rewards. Improvements in affairs.

Music: Happy times ahead.

Nails: Metal: Hard work is ahead. Difficulties to overcome. Finger nails: Quarrels and financial difficulties.

Necklace: Happiness and fun.

Nest: A windfall.

Net: Financial improvement and a raise in status.

Nuts: Problems will soon be solved.

Oak tree: Parting from a friend.

Opals: Happiness in love.

Oranges: Happiness and pleasure.

Palace: Sorrow for a friend.

Palm tree: The dreamer's dearest wish will come true.

Pin: Guard against a loss of status or a loss of face.

Pipe: An argument.

Plough: Respect and reward for good work.

Pond: Stagnation in affairs.

Purse: Full: Slight loss. Empty: Unexpected gain.

Race: The dreamer will soon be ahead of others.

Railway station: A journey.

Rainbow: A brighter future.

Razor: A quarrel brings unhappiness.

Road: Work brings rewards.

Rocks: Temporary difficulties.

Rose: Social success.

Scissors: A quarrel and the loss of a friend.

Sea: Calm: Happiness. Stormy: Anger.

Shooting star: Success in every way.

Sky: Wishes will shortly be fulfilled. Night sky: Temporary difficulties. Stormy sky: Great changes in the dreamer's way of life.

Smoke: A bad business transaction incurring losses.

Spectacles: The dreamer's self-esteem will take a knock.

Stairs: Improvement and change in circumstances.

Sun: Success in exams, business, or anything else.

Sword: Success, but the dreamer must guard against jealousy or attack by others.

Table: Improvement in health.

Tent: Unaccustomed activities.

Thorn: The dreamer will bring unhappiness to another.

Thunder: Danger for the dreamer or a loved one.

Tower: Ambitions will be achieved.

Trees: Upright: Ambitions achieved. Felled or fallen: Parting from a loved one.

Treasure: Hopes will come to nothing.

Tunnel: Extreme danger. Someone close to the dreamer may be dying or there could be a real threat to the dreamer's health or life.

Umbrella: Open: Friends will be helpful. Closed: Prosperity in business.

Violin: Affairs of love will go well.

Volcano: Upheavals. Physical effort will need to be made.

Water: Clear: Good health and prosperity. Muddy: Danger from disputes. Hot: Unexpected danger.

Wheel: Change for the better. A journey.

Window: Open: Problems will be solved. Closed: Unexpected danger, but the dreamer should be safe.

Wine: Social events and celebrations.

Yacht: Improvement in status and changes for the better.

16

Tasseomancy

The art of reading tea leaves or coffee grounds—called tasseomancy—used to be very popular, but it went out of fashion for several years, as did playing card reading, and this was probably due to the massive rise in popularity of the Tarot as a means of telling fortunes. However, tea cup reading is slowly creeping back into people's consciousness once again. There are full sized books around that cover every possible symbol; indeed, I have written them myself. However, in the meantime, the following list shows many of the more obvious symbols—which may well be enough to cope with until you become more proficient.

Preparation

Use a tea cup and saucer rather than a mug or a small demitasse coffee cup. The shallow type of cup with a plain interior is best because patterns or a fluted shape will interfere with the reading. Ask your querent to drink the tea or coffee and then to swirl the remaining material around in the cup in a counterclockwise direction three times, using his left hand. Then ask him to gently place the cup upside down on the saucer. Either you or the querent should now slowly turn the cup three times in a counterclockwise direction, once again using the left hand.

Needless to say, you will need to use leaf tea rather than tea bags—and ground coffee rather than instant. There are no rules about the type of tea or coffee you choose to use, but perhaps the types with the larger leaves or grounds would be best. Herbal tea, fruit tea, or any kind of tea or coffee will work perfectly well if that is what you or your querent prefer to drink.

After this, turn the cup over, keeping the handle toward you, tilt it to a convenient angle and take a good look inside.

Location and Timing of Events

The handle represents the querent himself. Any leaves in that area of the cup show that events concerning him or that occur will be in or near his home. The opposite side of the cup refers to strangers and events that occur away from home.

Symbols that point toward the handle represent things that are approaching the querent, while those that point away from him indicate things that are moving away from him. This movement might be a matter of location, or it may be a matter of timing. The bottom of the cup shows sorrows and the top shows joys.

The rim of the cup represents the near future. The area half-way down signifies events that will occur within a few weeks or months, while the area close to the bottom suggests the more distant future. If there are any numbers visible, these may help with the timing of events. For instance, an anchor would suggest a journey, and if this were accompanied by the number three, it would tell of a journey to come in three months' time.

Some Tea Cup Lore

- If two full spoons are accidentally put into one saucer, there will be news of twins.

- If a spoon is accidentally placed upside-down on a saucer, there will be news of a close relative becoming sick.

- A single leaf floating on a full cup of liquid means that the querent will come into money.

- A single leaf that is stuck at the side of a full cup of liquid indicates that a stranger will soon enter the querent's life.

- Stalks represent people and the color and size of the stalk can be assessed for an indication of the general appearance of the person.

- Letters of the alphabet can show the names of people.

- A triangle is usually considered to be lucky. But if it is found at the bottom of the cup or with the apex pointing downward, there may be a spell of bad luck on the way, or perhaps something that has been all right up to now could suddenly become difficult.

- Squares represent protection or restriction. If a dangerous symbol, such as an arrow, appears *inside* a square, the querent will be protected from harm.

- Crosses denote sadness or troubles to be faced.

- Dots always symbolize money. If the dots are close to another symbol, they may be linked.

- When a mountain appears, the querent will soon need to make a major effort in life.

- Clouds indicate muddles and illusion.

- Clear straight lines denote happy journeys, while wavy or broken ones signify problems related to travel.

- If you are hoping to find a new lover, place a teaspoon in a saucer and drip liquid into it until it is full, while counting the number of drips that this takes. This will tell you how many months will go by before you find your new lover.

The Symbols

Acorn: The start of something that will grow and succeed. A long life and good fortune. If it is in the middle of the cup, this indicates an improvement in health, other positions mean an improvement in finances.

Airplane: Sudden journeys for the querent or for someone close to him. If the airplane is ascending, things are on the up and up, but if it is descending there will be unexpected trouble. If the plane is travelling toward the querent it may be that someone is traveling to see him.

Anchor: A good symbol. If near the rim of the cup, there will be success in career and true love. A wish will come true soon. If half-way down, a journey will be successful. If there are dots around the anchor, this will be very lucky indeed. If at the bottom of the cup, the querent will receive help from friends and he will overcome difficulties. Only if the symbol is partially covered does it indicate continued troubles.

Angel: Good news, signifying love, happiness, and peace. There may be spiritual help on the way. Any new project (especially the birth of a child) will be accompanied by good luck. If the symbol is close to the handle of the cup, the home area will be particularly happy.

Arch: A happy marriage, a fresh start, and unexpected benefits. A proposal of marriage is possible, while other pleasant but temporary situations become permanent.

Apple: A time of achievement, happiness, and success. Hopes and wishes will be fulfilled. At the bottom of the cup, over-indulgence or temptation.

Arrow: Bad news. If the arrow points toward the handle, bad news is coming to the querent. If it points away, the querent may be the bearer of bad news. Dots show that financial trouble is ahead.

Baby: This may indicate the birth of a child but also the birth of a new project. If at the bottom of the cup, the pregnancy or plans may miscarry.

Bag: If closed, the querent will be caught in a trap; if open, he will manage to escape.

Ball: Ups and downs in life. The querent will soon bounce back from problems, and there will soon be new opportunities opening up.

Balloon: Success, but the position will show whether this is imminent or not. The closer to the top of the cup, the shorter the time scale.

Basket: Social success, happiness, and good fortune in and around the home. This is usually a good omen, but an empty basket or one that is obscured by other symbols can indicate domestic problems ahead.

Bed: A neat bed signifies a tidy mind, rest, and peace but a rumpled bed suggests sleepless nights and worry.

Bees: This has a combination of meanings that are usually good. This indicates a busy time ahead, either at home, at work, or both. There will be family gatherings and visitors bringing good news. One or more bees also signal good news for business ventures, money, and status at work or in business. A beehive also indicates a busy time.

Bell: This says that important news is on the way, and this can sometimes be news of a wedding. If the bell is near the rim, there will be a promotion at work. If half-way up, there will be good news of a general nature. If near the bottom, there could be sad news. Two bells indicate great happiness and celebrations and any forthcoming marriage will be successful.

Bird: Flying birds mean travel and also good ideas that can be translated into money. If surrounded by a circle or a square, there may be a proposal. Standing birds suggest that plans will be held up, while birds in a group indicate business meetings. If caged, there will be obstacles and restrictions. If the bird is holding a branch there will be reconciliation. A bird's nest signifies security, and if there are eggs in it, there will be a "nest egg." A broken nest might indicate a broken home.

Boat: Protection from danger, a safe haven, or a safe journey. If the boat is capsized, there will be unreliable people and upsetting circumstances.

Book: Depending upon circumstances, a book can indicate studies, secrets, legal matters, or writing for a living.

Box: If open, a romantic problem will soon sort itself out. If closed, something that has been lost will turn up.

Broom: Time to clear out old problems and start afresh.

Butterfly: A fickle lover or a short-lived affair. If surrounded by dots, this will be costly.

Candle: Illumination, help from others, inspiration, enlightenment. A guttering candle says that someone close to the querent is becoming less important to him.

Cat: If the cat is pouncing, there will be treachery and false friends. If it is seated, there will be contentment and good luck.

Chair: A time to rest, visitors, or, with dots nearby, a financial improvement.

Chimney: If smoke rises up, things will go well but if it goes sideways the querent may soon be restricted or bored. No smoke, hidden danger.

Church: Help, safety, unexpected benefits.

Circle or ring: This is often a sign of an impending marriage. With dots, a baby—three dots indicating a boy. Two circles signify a hasty marriage that brings regrets or perhaps two marriages.

Coffin: Sad news, regret, loss, and an enforced decision to bring something to an end. Someone may leave the querent, but this may be a relief.

Crescent: A new interest and success in finances, a journey over water, and success for or through women. Changes may come about during a new moon. If the moon is accompanied by a star, this is an exceptionally lucky omen. A new moon indicates new interests and success in finances. Any crescent could indicate luck though dealings with women or travel over water.

Cross: Trouble, suffering, and worry and sad news if it is close to the rim.

Crown: Honors and success. With a star nearby, unexpected luck.

Cup: Success and fulfillment, especially in creative and emotional matters.

Dagger: A jealous person will make trouble. Also a warning against haste.

Devil: Passion, lust, a hectic love affair.

Dice: If bad omens are nearby, this is a warning against gambling. Otherwise, speculation should be all right.

Dog: If the dog is running and happy, there will be happy meetings. If sad or at the bottom of the cup, a friend will need help.

Dot: A single dot increases the importance of any symbol near it. Otherwise dots mean money.

Dragon: Unforeseen problems, major clashes and upheavals.

Drum: Arguments. If near the bottom of the cup there may be rumors and scandal attached to the querent. Otherwise a successful career involving the general public.

Duck: Money coming, luck in gambling, work connected to travel and foreigners.

Eagle: A change of address and a time to grasp opportunities.

Egg: A symbol of fertility. A fresh start and the birth of a project.

Elephant: A symbol of strength, wisdom, and a slow climb up the ladder of success. A good time for a new business or a new lover.

Envelope: Good news is on the way. A letter or number may give you a clue as to whom this is from.

Eye: The querent may learn something to his advantage soon, but be on guard against untrustworthy people.

Face: If this looks like someone the querent knows, this could be significant. Otherwise the omen is good if the face is smiling, not so good if it is sad or scowling.

Fan: A warning to keep something to oneself.

Fish: This indicates luck in anything the querent wishes to do. Travel, a move, or a lucky meeting with a foreigner is possible.

Flag: This is a good omen if backed up by other good omens, however if the flag is black or half mast, courage will soon be needed.

Fork in a road: A choice of pathways is ahead.

Frog: This is associated with the ancient Egyptian goddess Isis, and it foretells good luck, happiness, good friends, love, and protection from harm.

Gallows: The querent's judgement may not be reliable in the near future.

Gate: An opportunity.

Grapes: Grapes are associated with the ancient Greek god Dionysus or the Roman god Bacchus. So a good time should soon be had by all, but the querent will need to guard against deception.

Guitar: Social events that include music, romance, and relaxation.

Gun: Quarrels, violence, war, and even a threat of death by violence. If the gun is in the home area, that is where the danger will be, otherwise the querent must guard against mugging and so on. If the gun is at the bottom of the cup, there is a real threat of death by violence, terrorism, or war.

Hammer: There is much work to be done. Not all of it is pleasant but it must be tackled.

Hand: If the hand is pointing to the handle, a situation is likely to develop in the home, if it is pointing away from the handle, the situation will occur outside the home. If the hand is open, friends will be helpful, but if it shows a fist, the querent can expect a fight. Clasped hands signify friendships and agreements, while a clenched fist at the bottom of the cup indicates that the querent will need to keep his feelings under tight control. Thumbs up = go ahead. Thumbs down = wait.

Hat: A man's hat is an unlucky sign but a woman's hat is a fortunate one.

Heart: A symbol of love. A heart with arrows through it signifies a passionate romance, while dots nearby denote marriage to a wealthy partner. Two small hearts with leaves close by indicate a lover's tiff. If at the bottom of the cup, this can be a health warning.

Horse: The meaning depends upon what the horse is doing. If galloping, this means good news. If there is also a rider, the news comes from afar. A horse's head brings a faithful lover, but clouds around bring delays in romance.

Horseshoe: Good luck, good health, money coming.

House: If near the handle, there may be domestic trouble. If near the rim, there may be a change of address, but if on the side of the cup, this is temporary. If obscured or at the bottom of the cup, care will be needed at home and at work.

Island: A pleasant vacation.

Jug: If near the rim this means good health, but if near the bottom, this indicates extravagance and losses. Other positions indicate power, prosperity, and a position of importance.

Juggler: A good omen for work but a warning against being taken in by others.

Kettle: If near the handle, comfort and contentment in the home, but if accompanied by clouds or at the bottom of the cup, discord and ill health in the home.

Key: A change of address is possible. If double or at the bottom of the cup, a robbery is possible. Crossed keys bring authority and honor in public life, plus success in love. A bunch of keys indicates health, wealth, and happiness.

Kite: The querent is being advised to go ahead with schemes but to keep a realistic attitude.

Knife: Quarrels and separations. If near the handle, this seems to be a relationship or family matter, but if away from the handle, there may be a stab in the back at work. At the bottom of the cup, problematic legal problems. Otherwise there might be surgery, injections, and dental treatment. Crossed knives indicate violence while a broken knife suggests helplessness.

Knight in armor: A helpful man or a new lover for a female querent.

Ladder: Spiritual enlightenment and advancement at work. If rungs are missing, there will be setbacks, but if at the bottom of the cup, financial misfortune.

Lamp: Success, financial improvement, celebrations. Two lamps signify two marriages.

Luggage: A journey or even emigration.

Man: If facing toward the handle, this denotes a visitor, and if he had his arm stretched out, he will bring gifts. If facing away from the handle, the man could be leaving. If he is shown carrying bags, he is hard working.

Maypole: Fertility. This also indicates that spring will bring improvements.

Monk: A time for rest, retreat, and contemplation.

Moon: (See Crescent)

Mountains: Obstacles, but if the peeks are clear the querent will overcome them. With dots, financial success through hard work.

Mouse: Poverty, theft (especially if at the bottom of the cup). Missed opportunities.

Mushroom: A variety of meanings, including setbacks in business, expansion of the querent's horizons, a home in the country, and illusion.

Necklace: Love ties will be important and successful as long as the necklace is complete.

Oak tree: Strength, courage, and building something that will last. Happy marriage.

Owl: Gossip, scandal, and allegations.

Parachute: A lucky escape.

Parcel: A surprise.

Peacock: With a spread tail, buying land or property. If the image is clear of obstacles, this means luck in marriage, health, wealth, and happiness for the querent and his children. If at the bottom of the cup or obscured, disappointment from children and plans not working out.

Phoenix: Recovery, rebirth.

Pipe: Problems will be solved. Also a kind and loving man.

Pistol: Danger.

Policeman: Help from those in authority.

Poppy: Loss, sadness, sickness. If near the rim, there will be a rapid recovery.

Pyramid: Achievements, but they will need to be worked at.

Question mark: Caution will be needed.

Rainbow: Happiness and prosperity. Check where the rainbow ends.

Rat: Treachery, deceit, and loss.

Raven: Bad news, losses, sickness, sadness.

Ring: If complete, a wedding or a happy marriage.

Road: Check out the state of the road. If it is clear and direct, the future outlook is pleasant and easy, but if it is blocked, there will be problems. A fork in the road denotes choices.

Robin: An ancient symbol of death—so there may be a change of circumstances as a result of someone's death.

Rose: Success in creative enterprises, love, happy marriage. If at the bottom of the cup, some delays.

Scaffold: A warning to stay within the limits of the law.

Scales: Lawsuits. If the scales are balanced, the legal matters will turn out well; otherwise there will be loss and injustice.

Scepter: Honors and rewards.

Scissors: A separation, quarrels, and misunderstandings.

Shell: Good news, luck, and money. Luck in love and justice in legal affairs. A sign of rebirth, or a change in consciousness.

Ship: A journey will be lucky, especially if connected to business.

Signpost: See which symbol it points to, as this will be especially important.

Skeleton: Losses. The loss of a friend. Skeletons emerging from the closet.

Soldier: A powerful friend, but alternatively this could indicate hostility toward the querent.

Spade: Hard work followed by a successful result.

Square: Restriction and hardship but also protection from real harms.

Stairs: A rise in status at work and in other areas of life.

Star: A six-pointed star indicates good fortune while a five-pointed one increases spiritual awareness. Small stars close to the handle denote talented children while a large number of stars can denote sadness and loss, although finances would be unaffected. A single star at the bottom of the cup suggests that a change of direction is needed.

Sticks: Crossed sticks indicate quarrels and partings while leaves clustered around a stick indicate bad news. Dots or small leaves nearby suggest that someone will help financially and a ring nearby indicates a marriage.

Sun: Happiness, success, power, and influence. If obscured, pride will bring a downfall.

Swallow: A change for the better in every way. If close to the handle, the home life will improve, if away from the handle, this foretells a successful and happy trip.

Swan: Progress and contentment, but other possibilities include an interesting lover and an improvement in finances. If at the bottom of the cup, death or separation.

Sword: (See knife)

Table: Celebrations, meetings, new friends, and discussions of all kinds.

Tower: If the tower is whole, the querent is building something that will last. If it is incomplete, there will be failures or a change of direction.

Train: A fortunate journey.

Tree: Recovery from sickness, ambitions fulfilled.

Umbrella: If this is open, there may be a new home. If closed, the querent may not be able to have this. If inside out, the querent is responsible for his own problems.

Unicorn: A secret marriage.

Van: Business travel or deliveries, packages arriving or a move of premises.

Vase: A friend will need the querent's help.

Violin: Popularity, success, fun, and entertainment.

Volcano: Passion or arguments—or both.

Wall: A time to overcome obstacles and build for the future.

Web: Being caught up in an embarrassing or awkward situation.

Whale: Success in a large project.

Wheel: Progress and changes for the better. Success, travel, and achievements. If at the bottom of the cup, the querent must curb impulsiveness.

Wolf: Jealousy and swindles. This can be a lucky sign if the querent's children are sick as it denotes recovery for them.

Woman: If the symbol is clear, there will be harmony and happiness, but if obscured there may be a jealous or spiteful woman around.

Yacht: An easier life, possibly due to retirement.

Zebra: Travel, possibly even a wandering lifestyle. The querent may soon have a secret love affair, which will be pleasant—as long as it remains a secret.

17

Witch Doctor's Bones

Some years ago, a friend brought me a small witch doctor's kit of the type that is sold in tourist shops in South Africa. This contained two bones that had clearly once been part of a chicken's leg and four small ones that had been part of the poor chicken's feet; also several small semi-precious stones and two large seeds. Several years later, I visited South Africa myself and I treated myself to another set of witch doctor's bones. People occasionally ask me to throw the bones as a kind of party piece, and when I do so, I find that they work extremely well. These tourist packs are a smaller version of exactly the same kind of bone, stone, and seed kit that real sangomas (witch doctors or shamans) use. The bones appear to work partly by a system that designates a meaning to each bone, stone, or seed and partly by opening the reader up to clairvoyant impressions.

The bones

Of the two main bones in the chicken's leg, the larger bone represents a male figure, and the smaller one represents a female figure. The four smaller bones can represent children or creative ventures. Two of the stones are brick-red pieces of polished jasper, and these are said to denote evil influences, bad luck, sickness, and other misfortunes. The two other stones are beautiful golden-brown striped stones, that are known as tiger's eye. These are said to show good influences that emanate from the querent himself due to common sense and any efforts that he makes on his own behalf. The two large seeds represent the wisdom of the ancients, which can be good influences from ancestors and spiritual guides or perhaps the collective wisdom of the tribal elders.

You can create your own kit by saving and cleaning the bones from roasting chicken.

The method

The instruction leaflet suggests that two parallel lines about two to three inches apart should be scratched into the ground with a stick. Then the sangoma sits opposite the querent, makes a small prayer to his spiritual guides, and then throws the bones, stone, and seeds gently onto the ground. Any object that falls inside the two lines represents people and situations that are close to the querent, also current events or those that will take place in the near future. Items that fall outside the lines represent people and situations that are at a distance from the querent or events that are further away into the future. The further away the object, the more distant the time.

I discovered that the best way to read the bones was to start at the upper left hand side and work down to the lower right hand side. I since discovered that this is a common procedure among people who read crystals and stones here in the West.

18

Tarot Cards

Tarot cards are no longer the mysterious objects that they once were, although there are still plenty of people who have never consulted a Tarot reader or been given a reading by a friend who knows how to do it. If you have just acquired a Tarot deck and you are new to the system, this is what you do. Shuffle your cards many times in order to remove their newness and also to mix them up well. Before using the cards for the first time, mentally ask for your cards to give help and guidance to yourself and others and to bring good luck to all who consult them. Once you have done this, try them out for yourself once or twice but then look around for a couple of guinea pigs to test them out on as soon after this as possible. At this point, it would also be worth scanning your local book shop or the Internet for a few books on the subject. My own book, *Fortune Telling by Tarot Cards*, is designed for beginners, and the feedback that I have had from this tells me that people find it clear and easy to understand. In the meantime, here is some basic information that will get you off the ground.

The Tarot deck

A Tarot deck is composed of two sections, the Major Arcana and the Minor Arcana. The Major Arcana is a set of twenty-two cards that are both powerful and completely individual in that they don't link with any other cards. The Minor Arcana is a set of fifty-six cards that are arranged in four suits, much like a deck of playing cards. (Playing cards evolved from the Tarot.) Each suit contains an Ace, cards that are numbered from two to ten, then a Page, Knight, Queen, and King. The suits are called Cups, Wands, Coins, and Swords. Some decks use different names, so it is common to find the suit of Wands called Rods or Staves and the suit of Coins called Pentacles, due to the pentacle shaped design on the coins in those decks.

When you have shuffled and laid out the cards, you may notice that some of them are the upside down. At this point, I suggest that you simply turn these cards the right way up. Some readers use reversed cards and assign a different meaning to them, which is often a weaker version of the upright card meaning. However many readers use the cards only in the upright position, so I suggest that for the time being you do the same.

The Major Arcana

Many of the powerful Major Arcana cards signify new beginnings, turning points, and major events, but it is sometimes difficult to assess what these might be, so it is the Minor Arcana cards that surround these cards that usually throw light on the subject. The ratio of cards in a Tarot deck is two thirds Minor Arcana to less than one third Major Arcana, so if more than one third of the reading contains Major Arcana cards, you can be sure that fate is controlling the person's destiny. If less than a third of the cards in a reading are from the Major Arcana, the chances are that the person is in charge of his own destiny at the time of the reading.

The Minor Arcana

Each suit is related to a different aspect of life. Cups represent emotional situations or an emotional reaction to something, along with creativity and matters of affection. Wands represent day-to-day activities and such things as one's job, communicating with others, dealing with minor hassles, travel, household issues, and all the usual running around and coping with life that we all have to do. Coins represent resources, and these may signify income, finance, property, land, a farm, a business, a career, and practical matters as a whole. Swords represent ideas and the need to take action, and often problem areas that are likely to arise.

It makes sense to assess the nature of the cards that turn up in a reading. For instance, if Cup cards dominate, you can be sure that the person's feelings about a situation will be paramount, and the reading itself may well concern romance, love, and relationships. If Wands dominate, then the person will be very busy. If Coins are the issue, then practical matters and such things as job security, finances, the value of a property, or something else of the kind is in the air. If Swords dominate a reading, storm clouds may be gathering and some kind of action needs to be taken.

The Court cards

Generally speaking, the King and Queen cards represent people in a reading. The Knights also represent people, but they can also indicate movement in one's affairs. The Pages tend to represent young people or those who are less important to the querent, but they often represent news and communications of various kinds. There are various ways of categorizing the Court cards, but the following makes life easy for a beginner:

- Kings signify mature men. Queens signify mature women, Knights signify younger men and the Pages signify younger women and children.

- Cups indicate emotional people who may be loving, easily upset, or short-tempered and they often represent people who affect our emotions.

- Wands represent friendly, competent people who communicate well and who are good to work with. They may have teaching ability, logic, and wisdom, but they may not be as passionate as we would like them to be.

- Coins denote practical people who can give us financial advice or fix things that are broken. They have great resources and much common sense but they may be a little dull when it comes to love and romance.

- Swords suggest exciting people who may stimulate us on an intellectual level or a sexual one, but they have an innate aggression or instability that can make life difficult for us. These people are wonderful to consult when professional or specialist advice is required and they can represent such types as doctors, lawyers and other professionals in our lives when this is appropriate.

If you are into astrology, here is another idea for you to play with. Cup cards represent water sign people. Wand cards represent fire or air sign people. Coin cards represent earth sign people, and Sword cards also represent fire or air sign people. Even if these cards don't actually link to a person's sun sign element (although they often do), they can express the character of those elements.

Spreads and layouts

There are many Tarot spreads, but as a beginner I suggest that you experiment with the following two ideas. The first will suit those of you who have a more intuitive approach, while the second will suit those who need more guidance or a more logical approach. There is no either/or situation here, you can try using both techniques. Both systems start off the same way.

Ask your querent to shuffle the cards and then give them back to you. Now lay out seven cards from the top of the deck and place them in a row in front of you. Note whether there are more than two Major Arcana cards, as this will tell you that your querent is in the hands of fate. Note which suit of the Minor Arcana predominates as this will tell you whether you are looking at an emotional situation, a financial or practical one, a fairly ordinary one, or something really difficult. See if there are any Court cards, because if these predominate, it shows that other people are a major factor in the life of your querent.

If you want to take an intuitive approach, simply look at the cards again and read them one by one from left to right, using the interpretations in this book. You can even use this as a crude timing device, as the first couple of cards will probably show the current situation, while the later one show how things will develop.

To make the second system work, you need to take eight small pieces of paper. Now write the word "relationships" on one piece of paper and put this down on the table. Write the word "money" on the second piece of paper and place that on your table. Now do the same for the other six, writing the words "health," "family," "property," "career," "other interests," and "potluck."

At this stage, you will have to ask your querent what his other interests might be. He may tell you that he is having problems with a neighbor or he may be in desperate need of a new car. He may be interested in some sport or hobby, he may have a journey on his mind, or he may be concerned about any one of a hundred other things. Once you know what this is, you will be able to apply the card to the reading. The potluck card will probably throw up something that neither of you has considered.

Now lay your seven cards out by placing each card above each piece of paper and read each card in the context of the situation that it falls into. For instance, if a card that talks of property matters falls in the property area, you can be sure that there will be a change of address or a positive outcome to a property matter. However, if it falls in a romantic or work area, then it is likely that a property, home, or place has some relevance to the reading. If this turns up in the pot-luck section, then the querent may not be concerned about a property matter at the time of the reading—but this may become an issue in his future.

If after this, you want more information on any matter, simply ask your querent to shuffle the cards again and read seven cards by the intuitive method but apply the whole seven-card layout to the specific question or situation. For instance, if you have picked up on a question of love and you want more information, a reading that is devoted to love alone will probably give you the answer.

Interpreting the Cards

Interpreting the meaning of the individual cards is an exhaustive subject area, much larger that can be contained in one chapter. The meanings I provide here are necessarily brief. My book *Fortune Telling by Tarot Cards* will give you much deeper meanings and many more alternative ideas than I can offer here.

The suit of Cups

Ace of Cups: The beginning of love, affection, and friend-ship. A gift, perhaps a ring. Joyful news, possibly the birth of a child.

Two of Cups: A successful relationship or happy partnership, possibly also a reconciliation.

Three of Cups: A wedding, either for the querent or for someone he cares about. Celebration, joy, childbirth, parties, and fun.

Four of Cups: Dissatisfaction because the querent may want more than he can have. This may be friendship when what he really wants is love. To some extent, a search for something new.

Five of Cups: Loss and sadness, but something remains from which the querent can begin to rebuild his life.

Six of Cups: Past skills and past associations will have meaning or become useful again in the future. Family gatherings and catching up with old contacts. Also contact with children or revisiting one's own childhood in some way.

Seven of Cups: There are many options available but the querent needs to use both logic and intuition to work out which is likely to be the best. If money is a stumbling block to romance, this will soon be overcome.

Eight of Cups: The end of a miserable time is in sight. Soon the querent will turn his back on past problems and move slowly forward.

Nine of Cups: Great satisfaction, but the querent must guard against smug-ness. Possibly marriage to a mature person.

Ten of Cups: Joy, happiness, happy family life. A birth is possible.

Page of Cups: A gentle, loving, and sensitive young woman or child. A time to study and reflect. Business matters will proceed slowly but surely.

Knight of Cups: A kindly, good-natured young man but he may be immature. Even an older man can be indicated here, but he will be ruled by immature emotions. Changes in relationships. A lover may travel soon. Slow changes in affairs.

Queen of Cups: A loving and very feminine woman brings love and comfort. She is kind and generous but may be materialistic and lazy.

King of Cups: A kindly, emotional man who cares for the querent. He has a complex character that makes him exciting but he can be dogmatic, difficult, and dictatorial. He is sensual, loving, and fond of children and of the good life.

The suit of Wands

Ace of Wands: The birth of an idea, a child, new possibilities, a rebirth of some kind.

Two of Wands: A partnership or relationship that is based on shared interests. Sometimes this indicates a move or perhaps a proud man who is around the querent.

Three of Wands: New projects, a new job, and good news. There may be travel in connection with work. Partnerships and relationships work well.

Four of Wands: Security and a feeling of putting down roots, and sometimes this refers to a new house with a bit of land around it.

Five of Wands: Challenges, but these can be dealt with successfully. Courage will be needed. Travel plans may be put on hold.

Six of Wands: Victory, achievement, earning a living. Problems will be overcome, delays will be ended and legal matters will succeed.

Seven of Wands: There is much to do, but if the querent takes one thing at a time in a logical order, he will succeed. There may be temporary problems relating to health, money, obstructive people, or other situations but they will soon pass.

Eight of Wands: Travel and new experiences will broaden the querent's horizons. Friendship and even love may be on the way.

Nine of Wands: The querent is now in a reasonably secure situation but he must stay alert. Most problems are behind him but he should remain prudent for a while longer.

Ten of Wands: There are many burdens and responsibilities but the effort is worthwhile.

Page of Wands: A bright and rather restless child. A journey, visitors, letters, writing, and phone calls. Property matters will go smoothly.

Knight of Wands: A friendly and intelligent man. An interest in communications work, or there may be contact with teachers. Visitors, moving, travel, and correspondence. A lively atmosphere.

Queen of Wands: A charming, clever woman who is a good companion; perhaps a clever businesswoman with a mind of her own. She may lack confidence, rush into things, or get irritated when hassled. She is sexy, loving, and a good friend.

King of Wands: An attractive man with a ready smile. Amusing and interesting, he is a good communicator and teacher. Helpful in a working relationship but a bit detached emotionally.

The suit of Coins

Ace of Coins: There is money coming or perhaps a new source of income. There may be a win, a bonus, or a raise in salary or status. Good news regarding money or a fresh start where funds and resources are concerned.

Two of Coins: A separation of resources. This may involve juggling time or money or borrowing to pay for something. Alternatively, putting money aside for some purpose or a division of funds due to divorce or a separation.

Three of Coins: Buying or renovating a property. Being given a job or a project to do. Using skills successfully and perhaps a fresh start connected to work or some project.

Four of Coins: Financial stability, stable resources, security. Perhaps too much emphasis on money for the querent's good.

Five of Coins: Loss, delays in payment, examination failure. Sometimes love goes well but finance is worrisome for a while.

Six of Coins: Money can be paid out or loaned out. The querent will be able to repay debts, finance a divorce, or help others who are worse off. He must guard against being drained by others.

Seven of Coins: Slow growth and steady achievement. Work that brings satisfaction and perhaps also monetary gain.

Eight of Coins: A new job, much work to be done, a creative endeavor, or a new skill to be learned.

Nine of Coins: Money and success are on the way. A good time to buy goods for the home or to start growing things. Home life will be happy.

Ten of Coins: Money, success, and pleasure from personal achievement. Travel in connection with work. A good marriage and happy family life. Setting up something that will last. A successful business.

Page of Coins: A steady, practical, business-like youngster. Good news about money or travel. Promotion or success.

Knight of Coins: A cautious young or immature man. News about business, money, or practical matters. Travel in connection with work.

Queen of Coins: A practical, businesslike woman; a skilled negotiator and good homemaker; a loving companion. May be rather materialistic.

King of Coins: A solid citizen, a financial advisor. A cautious and sensible man who needs financial and emotional security but may be somewhat tight-fisted. A kindly family man.

The suit of Swords

Ace of Swords: A new idea and perhaps a fresh start. A situation that needs thought and effort. Deep feelings will be aroused, possibly with some passion. Power and justice will be on the way soon.

Two of Swords: Stalemate. No change yet. The querent can't see where he is going yet.

Three of Swords: Loss, sadness, sickness, and blood.

Four of Swords: Rest and recuperation, recovery from illness or worries. Possibly a connection with a hospital, health clinic, dentist, or therapist that is due to the querent's work or for a good purpose.

Five of Swords: Quarrels, jealousy, and partings. The querent will need to stand up for himself, and perhaps also to accept a parting. Someone may leave the querent's circle.

Six of Swords: Travel over water, a journey that may bring a turning point. Moving into a new environment, moving away from trouble, even becoming some kind of refugee. A gradual improvement in circumstances.

Seven of Swords: The querent needs to move on, taking what he can and leaving what he cannot take or use in the future. This may be a literal move or a metaphorical one. Legal advice may be needed. In some circumstances this may indicate a robbery or fraud.

Eight of Swords: The querent is temporarily tied down and he cannot see how to escape. Perhaps he chooses to stay stuck.

Nine of Swords: Illness, worry, and family problems. Sometimes an issue related to mothers or motherhood is a cause of worry. Often the problems are less serious than they appear to be and the querent is advised to do something rather than dwell on them.

Ten of Swords: Treachery and betrayal, a stab in the back. Loss, death, divorce, the end of a situation, a collapse of plans.

Page of Swords: An active, sporty, intelligent child. The querent should keep his eyes open as there may be important events going on. News of an opportunity or news of an unexpected problem. A contract or document. Advice, possibly given in secret.

Knight of Swords: A tough, brave, and intelligent young man. However, he may be aggressive or rash. Arguments and disputes. Decisions that need to be taken. Medical or legal matters to be faced, or perhaps a journey that needs to be made on the spur of the moment.

Queen of Swords: A clever, sharp woman who may be highly qualified. She demands respect and can give cool, professional advice. Alternatively, a woman may be aggressive, hurtful, sarcastic, jealous, or untrustworthy.

King of Swords: A clever and well-qualified man or one who can fix things. Help from a specialist of some kind. Alternatively, an aggressive, unpleasant man.

The Major Arcana

These are stand-alone cards. They each have a basic meaning and also far deeper implications than I have room for in this book. If one Major Arcana card confuses you, try taking another card from the deck and see if the combination of two cards can offer more information.

0. The Fool

A new chapter is about to open up, and this may take the querent into unfamiliar territory. Whatever it happens to be, the querent will be spiritually protected.

1. The Magician

The querent is about to tackle something new, but this is not something that is so far out of his experience that it leaves him floundering. He has the skills and experience to do this. This can sometimes indicate self-employment or the start of a business, but it could apply to spiritual work or indeed, any other kind of matter. In a woman's reading, this can indicate the arrival of an important new man.

2. The High Priestess

This stands for a mental approach where emotions can only cloud the issue. A combination of brains and intuition will be needed. Teaching or studying may become important and an instructor or advisor may turn up when he or she is wanted. For those who work in a spiritual field, this indicates that there is more work to come or that a practical job will need a spiritual slant.

3. The Empress

There will be fruitfulness and abundance, fulfillment and contentment. The querent can look forward to a happy marriage and children. Sometimes this indicates a move to a nice place that has some land around it. There will be emotional and financial security. Sometimes a mother figure proves to be helpful.

4. The Emperor

The querent will soon be in control of his situation and he may achieve a position of power either at work or within the family. Sometimes this refers to a boss, a father figure, or to the man in a woman's life, and, if so, this person should be reliable and successful.

5. The Hierophant

A teacher, guru, or spiritual advisor may soon help the querent. Advice and help will be forthcoming. The querent is advised to avoid anything illegal or dangerous and to keep to the traditional, straight and narrow path. It would be best if the querent sticks to convention and tradition in the future.

6. The Lovers

This card often indicates that some kind of choice needs to be made, and it is important for the querent to bear in mind that the outcome of his decision will affect those around him. Love affairs and relationships will soon be important. A working partnership or cooperative venture will succeed. The querent will soon improve his dress and appearance and make his surroundings attractive.

7. The Chariot

The querent has some kind of battle or project on his hands, but he should be able to deal with this successfully. Sometimes this card refers to travel or to the purchase or maintenance of a vehicle.

8. Justice

In some decks, the Justice card is placed in the number eleven position, in others it is number eight, as it is shown here. The meaning is quite simple because it shows that justice, fair play, and a balanced outcome is the right one. If the querent has a legal matter or any other matter where a fair outcome is needed, this will occur. Balance must be sought.

9. The Hermit

This indicates that the querent needs to take some time out from the hustle and bustle of daily life and do some thinking. He needs to retreat and reflect in order to obtain a clearer picture of what is needed.

10. Wheel of Fortune

This one is simple because all it means is that a change is on the way. If you lay out your row of cards and count them off as weeks or months, the position that this card falls in will show you when the change will come about.

11. Strength

This card appears as number eight in some decks rather than as number eleven as it is shown here. If the querent is sick, he will soon be feeling much better. If he has been in a weak position, this will also change for the better. This card implies gentle strength rather than aggression—so tact, diplomacy, a calm attitude, and a certain amount of endurance will be required.

12. The Hanged Man

The first meaning for this complex card is suspension. The querent may be anxious for something to happen immediately, but when this card shows up, the chances are that he will have to wait a while longer. The second meaning is of sacrifice, in the sense that in order to for one to have one thing, another needs to be sacrificed. For instance, the querent may have to give up some of his free time in order to get something done. A third meaning is that of initiation, in the sense that nobody can understand someone else's problems until they have been through something similar themselves. Therefore, in its way, this is a card of enlightenment.

13. Death

This is the dreaded death card that frightens those who are new to the Tarot. In my experience it never foretells the death of the querent, although it can indicate the death of someone around him if appropriate. However, its true meaning is that of transformation, in the sense that nothing stays the same forever. If the querent is wondering whether something is coming to a conclusion or whether something is really over, the answer is that it is—and that there will be no road back.

14. Temperance

This card talks of moderation in all things and of a time of peace. There will be a good balance between the various sides of the querent's life and for once everything will go well.

15. The Devil

This is another card that frightens newcomers to the Tarot, but it denotes bondage to something that is outmoded or that is no longer really valid. Unpleasant emotions like jealousy, rage, guilt, hanging on to the past or to a situation that is no longer working are all issues that need to be addressed. A practical rather than an emotional attitude will be needed. There may be a commitment to something healthy, such as a mortgage or a period of study, but the implications must be considered. Spiritual enlightenment may be on the way soon.

16. The Tower

Some decks call this The Struck Tower, and it is another unpleasant card. It frequently suggests that a shock or upheaval is on the way, and as this is likely to be unexpected, it can take some dealing with. Whether the upset is large or small, it can't be ignored. Sometimes there is an element of enlightenment, as at least the querent will know what has been going on, which means that he can do something about it. The Tower is a structure, so this card can refer to a problem that concerns the structure of the querent's home or business premises.

17. The Star

This is often called The Star of Hope, as it foretells a better time ahead when hopes and wishes will come true. The querent may learn something new or become wiser in the future. It can indicate study, travel, or widening of horizons.

18. The Moon

The querent is being faced with a situation where he cannot see daylight, or where he cannot see the forest for the trees. Nothing is clear and it is hard for him to make reasoned judgements. In romantic matters, it shows that nothing is what it seems. In any circumstance, lies, half-truths, and mysteries abound. Sometimes this indicates a problem for a mother figure.

19. The Sun

This is a card of joy and success. A love affair will go well, a marriage will be happy, a business venture will succeed. If appropriate, the querent will pass an exam or a test of some kind. Children and anything that relates to them will bring joy and happiness.

20. Judgement

The querent will be rewarded for his efforts. If he has been struggling with something for a while, it will work out to his satisfaction. He will be rewarded for past work and he will feel content with himself. Ideas and projects that have been shelved will come alive soon.

21. The World

Something is working its way to a conclusion and there will soon be space and time for something new to take its place. Sometimes this is a card of travel and expansion of horizons. Sometimes it just means that a phase of life will reach its natural conclusion, in readiness for something new.

19

Predictive Astrology

strology, like Tarot, is another subject much too vast to adequately cover in one chapter. There are many excellent books on the subject of astrology. The horoscopes you see in a newspaper or magazine are only the tip of a *huge* iceberg. You can be sure that the astrologer who writes the column knows a great deal, although little of this is reflected by what you see in the paper. Astrology can be used as an incredibly accurate form of psychoanalysis, for assessing the viability of love relationships, business partnerships, and political regimes, and for picking the best time to start a project or to track the outcome of an illness. Astrology is not hard to learn and anyone can get a grasp of the basics quite quickly. However, if you want to become proficient, you will need to take some courses and buy books and computer software that will enable you to produce modern horoscope charts. Having said all that, here is a quick overview of the way that predictive astrology works.

Newspaper astrology

Newspapers and magazines work with a method is called "sun sign astrology" or "solar house astrology," because the sign that the sun appears in at birth is treated as the first astrological "house."Almost everyone knows their birth sign (the sign of the zodiac on the birth date). The following illustration shows a basic horoscope chart, with the signs arranged around the zodiac wheel in their natural order, in their natural house placement. The

signs of the zodiac are always arranged in a counterclockwise direction around the chart, and the first house is always on the left hand side, as shown.

The sun has a regular pattern with the only variation being the exact time or date upon which it changes from one sign to the next during any particular year. This predictability means that even a nonastrologer can make a start on predicting his future trends. The chart below shows where the sun will be during any year (with minor variations at the cusp of each sign).

♈	Aries	March 21 to April 19
♉	Taurus	April 20 to May 20
♊	Gemini	May 21 to June 21
♋	Cancer	June 22 to July 22
♌	Leo	July 23 to August 22
♍	Virgo	August 23 to September 22
♎	Libra	September 23 to October 23
♏	Scorpio	October 24 to November 21
♐	Sagittarius	November 22 to December 21
♑	Capricorn	December 22 to January 19
♒	Aquarius	January 20 to February 18
♓	Pisces	February 19 to March 20

The time and place of your birth are crucial to establishing your accurate birth chart. Thus, one Virgo may have a first house sun placement, and another Virgo will have a sixth house placement. A professional astrologer can prepare your birth chart, which will provide amazing insight into your personality, your strengths, and your potential. This chapter will show you an easy predictive technique based on your sun sign.

Easy Predicting

Using the system that the newspapers employ, draw a circle and divide it into twelve "houses," with the first one on the left side as shown earlier in this chapter. Put your sun sign in the first house and write all the other signs in order around the side in an counter-clockwise direction. Therefore, if your sign is Gemini, that will be your first solar house. Cancer will be your second house, Leo your third, and so on until you reach Taurus, which will be your twelfth house.

Now it is a matter of working out which house the sun will be in during any month of the year. Once you have done that, consult the interpretation below to see what happens when the sun appears to move through any one of your houses. Naturally, there is far more to predictive astrology than this, but this is something that you can do for yourself without studying astrology at all.

The first house

The energy level rises.

This represents a fresh start, the beginning of something new or simply a more optimistic attitude. If you have been hanging back from something, you will take matters into your own hands and put things into action. This is a very masculine house, so it shows assertion—but also such things as speed, male-dominated jobs or tasks, and political ambition.

The second house

What's it worth to me?

The second house concerns anything that is of value to a person. This may mean money, income, resources, and personal possessions, but it also relates to the lifestyle that a person values, his main priorities, and also his self-image. To some extent this rules love and relationships, especially when land, property, farming, and goods are involved in the equation. This house is associated with artistic and musical interests and any attraction to work or the world of beauty, fashion, and glamour.

The third house

Talk, talk, talk.

This house signifies the ability to learn, speak, write, deal with foreign languages, communicate, and negotiate with others. It rules messages, errands, and the panoply of modern machinery that is involved with information technology. In addition, it is concerned with a subject's vehicle or any other means of local travel. Neighbors, siblings, and young people, such as nephews and nieces, and some friendships are shown here, as are sports, games, and youthful occupations.

The fourth house

Home is where the mortgage is.

This rules the home and property, including a person's business premises. It symbolizes domestic life, the roots, background, family history, and security. This relates to the mother, any mother figure, and family commitments. It can rule females in general and female products or services, and has a connection with the feminine aspect of giving help and service to others. It can rule tasks that involve dealing with the public.

The fifth house

Creating anything, including havoc.

Children and their education are found here, as are fun, holidays, games, and leisure pursuits, including some sports, dancing, singing, writing, and entertainment—especially if it contains a touch of glamour. This house denotes creativity and bringing things into being, including childbirth and business enterprises. Even publishing can be seen here if the person uses it to make a personal statement. Flirtation and love affairs that are meant to be fun can be seen here.

The sixth house

Work and health.

This house is associated with our daily work and daily chores. It also relates to the whole business of employing people and being employed, and the services that we perform for others. This is different from the tenth house, which may also relate to the career. However, the tenth house would be in the sense of the status and wealth that this brings, rather than the actual functions that we perform in our daily lives. Health matters are still very much concerned with the sixth house.

The seventh house

Love and hate.

This house rules open relationships such as marriage, partnerships, and working partnerships. Legal arrangements, cooperation, and pulling together are signified here. However, this house also rules open enemies. This is concerned with beauty, art, music, leisure, lovemaking, and pleasure.

The eighth house

Hatch, match, and dispatch.

The eighth house is also connected to the idea of partnership but in a more serious manner because it rules shared resources, shared financial matters, legally binding business arrangements, and unions of all kinds. Thus sex and resultant childbirth can be shown here—as can death. This house rules anything that is hidden from view, including secrets, crime, interests that are not broadcasted to others, and anything that is actually under the ground, such as coal, oil, gold, and other such resources. This house represents crime and investigation, forensic matters, and also cutting and gouging, as in surgery or even butchery.

The ninth house

To boldly go.

This house expands a person's horizons, so it is concerned with further or higher education, foreign travel, foreign goods or foreign people. Also exploring legal boundaries; searching for the truth of a matter; and exploring religious, philosophical, and spiritual ideas. It is about discovering what a person needs to believe in.

The tenth house

The ladder of success.

If you have drawn the design properly, you will see that this house starts at the top of the chart, therefore it rules a person's aims and aspirations. It is often taken to mean the job or career, but it really means the search for status and position in any sphere—even if this means having a more impressive television than the neighbors. This rules achievements, fame, public acclaim, and sometimes public disgrace. It is concerned with fathers and father figures.

The eleventh house

Detached relationships.

This is the house of acquaintanceship, friendship, group activities, clubs, and partying with friends. It rules intellectual pursuits and hobbies and original ideas or inventions. It can apply to teaching and learning, especially if the person is exploring ideas rather than getting a basic education. The eleventh house rules eccentricity, but also desire for change and even for revolution. It is especially associated with unexpected events and sudden upheavals. It can refer to stepchildren and adopted children.

The twelfth house

The inner world.

This rules a person's private place and his inner thoughts and feelings. It encompasses such things as fears, sorrows, and self-undoing, but it also rules a love of art, music, and creativity. Hidden talents, hidden lovers, and much else that is not obvious to outsiders are tucked away here. This house represents escapism—sometimes into alcohol or drug addiction, but also to places of seclusion, such as hospitals, prisons, a monk's cell, and the shed at the bottom of one's garden. However, along with such unpleasant matters as karmic debts, it also rules kindness and good deeds both given and received, especially if this is done quietly.

20

Palmistry

Palmistry is what people first think of when they hear the term "fortune telling." Not only is it the most universally understood method of fortune telling, it may well be the oldest. Hand reading is not an easy subject to pick up in the way that some other divinations are. It takes years of study to become even an adequate hand reader, and a lifetime to become a really good one.

The following pages will give you an introduction to the art of hand reading, but you need to buy several books and then look at as many hands as you can and then check your findings with their owners.

The three major lines

The illustration on page 179 shows the heart line, the head line, and the life line.

The life line

A strong life line shows health, strength, and the ability to bounce back from illness, but it doesn't necessarily show the length of life. A short or broken life line often "moves" across to some other part of the hand. This indicates a major change in life, such as divorce, emigration, major career changes and much else. A lifeline that clings around the thumb shows a home-loving person who prefers a stable job that keeps him in one place and a desire to put family life first. A life line that travels out across the hand signifies a more adventurous, career-minded person who loves to travel and who needs personal freedom. Forks on the line indicate that the person wants both options.

Disturbances on the line can indicate health problems and life events. If these disturbances are close to the top of the line, the neck will be affected, if they are closer to the lower end of the line, the lumbar or sacral area will be affected.

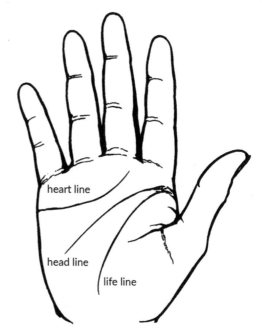

A person who is destined to live a long life will have at least some lines at the top of the hand, while a person who remains active until the end will have many of these. Take care when reading the hands of young people, because these lines don't all form until well into adulthood—sometimes even later. This shows that a person's fate is not necessarily written in the hand, and that personal choices and changes in circumstances can affect one's destiny.

The head line

Some palmists call this the line of intelligence. It shows how the person's mind works, and to some extent the kind of career choice they will make. A short line suggests that the person is either a specialist in his subject or that he has few interests. A line that extends across the hand or that wanders diagonally downward shows a lively mind and many interests. A horizontal line indicates a logical mind that is suited to practical tasks such as math or computing, while a sloping one is more suited to working for or with others and that the mind is more open to music, poetry, and romance. Once again, bends, breaks, islands, or disturbances on the head line can indicate specific health problems or changes in the career path.

The heart line

This shows the way a person feels, and to some extent the path of his love life. If the line is deep, curving, and bold, the person is able to give and receive love, and while his love life may or may not run smoothly, he will certainly have one! A curved line that reaches up to the fingers belongs to a true romantic who selects his partner almost on impulse and mainly because he loves, desires, and is fascinated by that person.

A straight line that runs horizontally across the hand indicates caution. This person chooses a partner based on race, religion, social status, educational background, financial background, or for some other practical purpose. This doesn't mean that the subject cannot love his chosen partner, but that he would find it hard to go against his mental programming for anything other than a quick fling. Many people have a forked line which shows that they could be attracted to a partner for either of the above reasons, or both.

Attachment lines

A person's attitude toward important relationships, and to some extent the number and progress of his love relationships, can be seen on the side of the hand, as per the illustrations below. These used to be called marriage lines but these days any strong attachment will apply.

It would be easy to read a person's future if one line meant one partnership, two lines meant two and so on, but this is not quite the case. The following shows you some of the options.

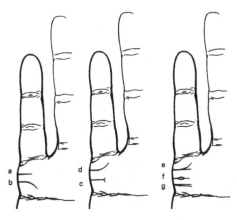

One strong line (a) shows a person who wants to attach to one person and stay with them for life—and it can mean that they do just that. However, if it cannot be so, they will find someone else and try to do the same with them.

Two lines (g) suggest that the person will not ignore relationship problems. If they become too severe, the person won't hesitate to leave and start looking around for someone new.

One strong line, or perhaps two strong lines and one or two weaker ones suggest several potential mates, but only one or two serious ones.

A young person who is not ready to settle down or someone who tried a relationship but prefers playing the field may have many weak lines. If their circumstances and outlook changes, one of these lines will strengthen and the others will fade away.

Obviously the clearer and cleaner these lines are, the more straightforward the person's situation. Here are a few possibilities:

- A clear line (a) denotes a relationship that is basically sound. A messy line denotes problems.

- A drooping line (b) shows that the subject's partner is nagging, dominating, or bullying the subject.

- A broken line shows parting and coming back together.

- A fork (e) represents problems that might or might not end in divorce.

- An "island" (f) suggests that the partner is temporarily suffering bad health.

Child lines

These are difficult to spot, so you need to look for them in a very good light. Try dotting a little talcum powder, face powder, or powdered eye-shadow on this area of the hand, as this can help to make these lines clear.

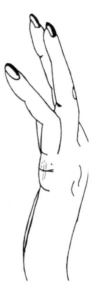

The child lines must cross through at least one attachment line for the child to be part of the subject's life. In theory, one line indicates one child, two lines indicate two children and so on, but a line can also indicate a good relationship with a stepchild so this doesn't always indicate childbirth. Miscarriages and abortions don't usually create a long or strong line, but if the person doesn't forget the lost child, the line can sometimes appear like the line for a living child. Some people have lines but no children. These subjects may look after children or even animals. If there are no child lines, the person may choose not to have children, may not be able to have them, may never have any dealings with children—or children are so far into their future that the lines have not yet formed.

The fate line

The fate line runs roughly up the middle of the hand. It is not easy to assess because it can rise from the life line, the bottom of the hand or the side that is away from the thumb. There can be a section of line at the lower end of the hand that peters out later or one that only starts fairly high up the hand.

The fate line can run toward the index finger, or toward the middle finger, as in the illustration. It rarely runs to the ring finger but it can throw branches in that direction. If it rises from the life line, as per the second illustration, the subject's family will help him to make a good start in life. If from the outer (percussion) side of the hand, other people will help him.

- A long straight fate line suggests a well-defined fate and a person who does his duty according to the society that he lives in, but he may never strike out for independence or discover who or what he really is.

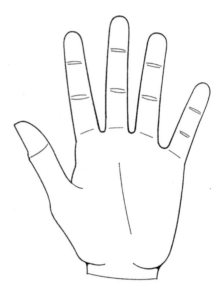

- A messy line with breaks, branches, accompanying lines, islands, bars across it and deviations of any kind represent a more interesting but less secure lifestyle.

- A fate line that starts early and then peters out shows a change of direction and perhaps a less defined sense of direction after the line ends.

- A fate line that starts late suggests that it will take time before the person has a clear idea of where he wants to go in life.

- A fate line that travels toward the index finger suggests determination, ambition, self-belief, and success in life.

- A fate line that travels toward the middle finger suggests that the person needs to work hard in order to provide for himself and others, but that success and a high level of status can be achieved.

- The line rarely goes in the direction of the ring finger, but if it throws a branch in that direction, the person can expect a nice home and a good deal of fun later in life.

- Islands on the line indicate times of confusion, financial problems, relationship troubles, and possible periods of ill health.

- Breaks denote breaks in the run of a person's life. If the line breaks and jumps to the thumb side, a change of career can be indicated. If it jumps to the percussion side, the person may pay less attention to a career or even give up work in order to concentrate on home life.

- Lines that join the fate line denote major influences in the person's life. This can indicate lovers, marriage partners, business partners, or indeed anybody who has an impact on his life.

- Parallel lines or a long island on the line show that the person's resources and energies are split—often between work and family or some other consideration.

Needless to say, there is much more to palmistry than this, and every single part of the hand, including the back of the hand and the fingernails has a story to tell. Hands are also wonderful maps to a subject's state of health, state of mind, and his life as a whole.

If this tiny introduction to this fascinating subject leaves you wanting more, seek out books on the subject listed in further reading.

Further Reading

A Little Book of Dream Symbols, by Jaqueline Towers (Hampton Roads Publishing, 2016)

Astrology Plain & Simple, by Cass and Janie Jackson (Hampton Roads Publishing, 2016)

Body Reading Plain & Simple, by Sasha Fenton (Hampton Roads Publishing, 2016)

Chakras Plain & Simple, by Sasha Fenton (Hampton Roads Publishing, 2017)

Chinese Astrology Plain & Simple, by Jonathan Dee (Hampton Roads Publishing, 2017)

Face Reading Plain & Simple, by Jonathan Dee (Hampton Roads Publishing, 2018)

Fortune Telling with Playing Cards, by Jonathan Dee (Hampton Roads Publishing, 2018)

Fortune Telling with Tarot Cards, by *Sasha Fenton* (Hampton Roads Publishing, 2017)

Handwriting Analysis Plain & Simple, by Eve Bingham (Hampton Roads Publishing, 2018)

I Ching Plain & Simple, by Kim Farnell (Hampton Roads Publishing, 2016)

Learning the Tarot, by Joan Bunning (Weiser Books 2019)

Lucid Dreaming Plain & Simple, by Robert Waggoner and Caroline McCready (Conari, 2015)

Modern Palmistry, by Sasha Fenton and Malcolm Wright (Hampton Roads Publishing, 2018)

Numerology Plain & Simple, by Anne Christie (Hampton Roads Publishing, 2016)

Palmistry Hand in Hand, by Beleta Greenaway (Hampton Roads Publishing, 2018)

Palmistry Plain & Simple, by Sasha Fenton (Hampton Roads Publishing, 2016)

Reading the Runes, by Kim Farnell (Hampton Roads Publishing, 2018)

Runes Plain & Simple, by Kim Farnell (Hampton Roads Publishing, 2016)

Super Tarot, by Sasha Fenton (Hampton Roads Publishing, 2015)

Talk to the Hand, by Vernon Mahabal (Weiser Books, 2015)

Tarot Mysteries, by Jonathan Dee (Hampton Roads Publishing, 2015)

Tarot Plain & Simple, by Leanna Greenaway (Hampton Roads Publishing, 2017)

Tea Cup Reading, by Sasha Fenton (Hampton Roads Publishing, 2018)

Tea Leaf Reading, by Jaqueline Towers (Hampton Roads Publishing, 2017)

The Hidden Zodiac, by Sasha Fenton (Hampton Roads Publishing, 2018)